Jürgen Beyerer, Alexey Pak (Eds.)

Proceedings of the 2016 Joint Workshop of Fraunhofer IOSB and Institute for Anthropomatics, Vision and Fusion Laboratory

Karlsruher Schriften zur Anthropomatik
Band 33
Herausgeber: Prof. Dr.-Ing. Jürgen Beyerer

Eine Übersicht aller bisher in dieser Schriftenreihe
erschienenen Bände finden Sie am Ende des Buchs.

Proceedings of the 2016 Joint Workshop of Fraunhofer IOSB and Institute for Anthropomatics, Vision and Fusion Laboratory

Edited by
Jürgen Beyerer and Alexey Pak

KIT Scientific Publishing

Impressum

KIT Scientific Publishing

Karlsruher Institut für Technologie (KIT)
KIT Scientific Publishing
Straße am Forum 2
D-76131 Karlsruhe

KIT Scientific Publishing is a registered trademark
of Karlsruhe Institute of Technology.
Reprint using the book cover is not allowed.

www.ksp.kit.edu

Print on Demand 2017 – Gedruckt auf FSC-zertifiziertem Papier

ISSN 1863-6489
ISBN 978-3-7315-0678-2
DOI 10.5445/KSP/1000070009

Preface

In 2016, the annual joint workshop of the Fraunhofer Institute of Optronics, System Technologies and Image Exploitation (IOSB) and the Vision and Fusion Laboratory (IES) of the Institute for Anthropomatics, Karlsruhe Institute of Technology (KIT) has again been hosted by the town of Triberg-Nussbach in Germany.

For a week from July, 24 to 29 the PhD students of the both institutions delivered extended reports on the status of their research and participated in thorough discussions on topics ranging from computer vision and world modeling to data fusion and human-machine interaction. Most results and ideas presented at the workshop are collected in this book in the form of detailed technical reports. This volume provides a comprehensive and up-to-date overview of the research program of the IES Laboratory and the Fraunhofer IOSB.

The editors thank Lars Sommer, Matthias Richter, and other organizers for their efforts resulting in a pleasant and inspiring atmosphere throughout the week. We would also like to thank the doctoral students for writing and reviewing the technical reports as well as for responding to the comments and the suggestions of their colleagues.

Prof. Dr.-Ing. Jürgen Beyerer
Alexey Pak, PhD

Contents

Combining YAWL and DBNs for Surgical Phase Detection

Patrick Philipp

Vision and Fusion Laboratory
Institute for Anthropomatics
Karlsruhe Institute of Technology (KIT), Germany
p.philipp@kit.edu

Technical Report IES-2016-01

Abstract: To provide assistance functions in context of surgical interventions, the use of a surgical phase detection plays an important role. By assessing the progress of an on-going surgery, a tailored (i.e., context sensitive) decision support for medical practitioners can be enabled. Subsequently, this provides opportunities to prevent errors, injuries, negligence or malpractices. In this work, a surgical phase detection, combining Yet Another Workflow Language (YAWL) with Dynamic Bayesian Networks (DBNs) is proposed. Thereby, YAWL is used to model the relationship of surgical phases; DBNs are used to allow for the detection of surgical phases of interest. The approach is presented for the application example of a cholecystectomy (removal of the gallbladder).

1 Introduction

In modern medicine, the use of assistance functions becomes increasingly important [PFHB16]. Such functions can be realized as part of a computer assisted surgery (CAS) to enable a decision support of the medical practitioners [KWN+15]. Thereby, a decision support opens up a scope of optimization: E.g. concerning the prevention of errors, injuries, negligence or (subsequently) malpractices.

In this context, a surgical phase detection plays an important role. Namely, because by assessing the progress of an on-going surgery, a tailored (i.e., context sensitive) decision support during an intervention can be enabled. In doing so, there is not only a passive dissemination (e.g. distribution via print media) of support (e.g. medical guidelines) – which was shown has only little effect on the actual practitioners behavior [FL92, SGM+11]. Instead, we propose to provide an interactive assistance in terms of a context sensitive decision support to assist medical practitioners during an intervention.

In this work, we focus on the application example of the removal of the gallbladder (cholecystectomy). Thereby, we consider the standard procedure of a cholecystectomy, the laparoscopic cholecystectomy. It is a minimal invasive approach using laparoscopes. These are endoscopes, specialized for an abdominal surgery (i.e. a surgery concerning the stomach). It is therefore not surprising that regarding CAS, the considered procedure can be categorized as a computer-assisted abdominal surgery [KWN+15].

This contribution is structured as follows: first, in sections 2 and 3, the fundamentals of Yet Another Workflow Language (YAWL) and Dynamic Bayesian Networks (DBNs) are presented. Section 4 gives details on the application example of a laparoscopic cholecystectomy and the according model in YAWL. Section 5 focuses on the modelling approach of combining YAWL and DBNS. The approach is verified in section 6 and, finally, a conclusion is drawn in section 7 on page 13.

2 Fundamentals on YAWL

There are various reasons for choosing YAWL (Yet Another Workflow Language) as a modeling tool for workflows [HRAA10]. One aspect is the expressive power reflected in various so called workflow patterns. Another aspect is the formal semantics which enable the application of analysis tools like WofYAWL [VvdAtH06] to verify a model.

Nevertheless, YAWL is said to be comprehensive [HRAA10], and building a valid model can be challenging task, especially if the medical expert uses YAWL on his own – and therefore without the assistance of a technical domain expert.

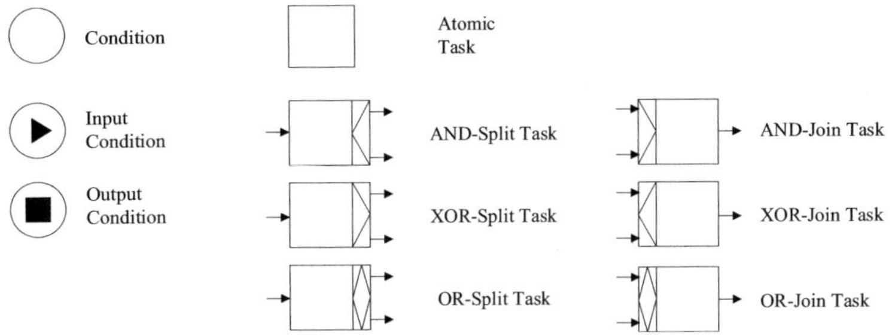

Figure 2.1: Important elements of the YAWL notation. A condition is represented by a circle and a task is represented by a square. There are two unique conditions: the so called input condition (black triangle in a circle) and the output condition (black square in a circle). A task can be expanded by a split and a join behavior which is indicated by the corresponding symbols.

Consequently, in [Phi16] we introduced translation rules transferring one comprehensible UML activity into a YAWL specification. That means, YAWL can be used as an intermediate language for further assistance functions which are build upon a YAWL specification.

Figure 2.1 depicts important elements of the YAWL notation. Since YAWL is an extension of so-called Workflow Nets [AH03], their elements show a high degree of similarity. Formally, a YAWL specification is a non-empty set of extended workflow nets (EWF Nets). Such an EWF Net can comprise several conditions which are represented by circles[1] (cf. Figure 2.1). Furthermore, an EWF Net comprises two unique conditions: one unique input condition, which is represented by a black triangle in a circle, as well as a unique output condition, which is represented by a black square in a circle (cf. Figure 2.1). A task of the EWF Net is given by a square, which can be expanded by a split and a join behavior (cf. Figure 2.1).

Formally, an EWF Net is given by the following tuple [VvdAtH06, HRAA10]:

$$EWF = (i, o, C, T, F, f_{\text{split}}, f_{\text{join}}, f_{\text{rem}}, f_{\text{nofi}}) ,$$

[1] Compared to Petri Nets, a condition can be interpreted as a place [AH03].

where

- $i \in C$ is the input condition,
- $o \in C$ is the output condition,
- C is a set of conditions,
- T is a set of tasks,
- $F \subseteq ((C \setminus \{o\}) \times T) \cup (T \times (C \setminus \{i\})) \cup (T \times T)$ is the flow relation,
- Every node in the graph $(C \cup T, F)$ is on a directed path from i to o,
- $f_{\text{split}} : T \rightsquigarrow \{\text{AND, OR, XOR}\}$ [2] specifies the split behavior of each task,
- $f_{\text{join}} : T \rightsquigarrow \{\text{AND, OR, XOR}\}$ specifies the join behavior of each task,
- $f_{\text{rem}} : T \rightsquigarrow \mathbb{P}^{+}(T \cup C \setminus \{i, o\})$ [3] specifies the tokens to be removed by emptying a part of the net,
- $f_{\text{nofi}} : T \rightsquigarrow \mathbb{N} \times \mathbb{N}^{\text{inf}} \times \mathbb{N}^{\text{inf}} \times \{\text{dynamic, static}\}$ specifies the multiplicity of each task.

In this work, we focus on the combination of a given YAWL specification with Dynamic Bayesian Networks (DBNs). Therefore we introduced the necessary basics of YAWL in this section and proceed with the fundamentals on DBNs in the following section.

3 Fundamentals on DBNs

There are many reasons for considering Dynamic Bayesian Networks (DBNs) [DK89] as a modeling tool for dynamic systems [Mur02]. With respect to the modeling of medical workflows, we opted for DBNs because they combine a reasonable tradeoff between expressiveness and complexity, and include probabilistic models that have proved to be successful in practice (e.g. Hidden Markov

[2] Please note: $\rightsquigarrow$ denotes a partial function. I.e., a task can have no specified split behavior, too.
[3] Please note: $\mathbb{P}^{+}(X)$ denotes the power set of X without the empty set: $\mathbb{P}^{+}(X) = \mathbb{P}(X) \setminus \{\emptyset\}$

Models) [LJ14]. Additionally, due to their factorized state space, DBN models allow improved modularity and interpretability. In contrast to a Hidden Markov Model, their state space can be expressed in a factored form and not only as a single discrete random variable. Furthermore, concerning Kalman Filter Models, DBNs allow for arbitrary probability distributions (not only for unimodal linear-Gaussians) [Pad10].

A Bayesian Network (BN) is a probabilistic graphical model (PGM), combining graph theoretic approaches with approaches of probability theory. Consequently, a BN over random variables $X^{0:N} := X^0, \ldots, X^N$ is given by a pair

$$B = (G, P)\,.$$

Whereby G corresponds to a directed, acyclic graph (DAG)

$$G = (V, E)\,, \quad \text{and} \tag{3.1}$$

$$P(X^{0:N}) = \prod_{n=0}^{N} P(X^n|\mathrm{Pa}(X^n))\,, \tag{3.2}$$

corresponds to a joint probability distribution [KF09]. DAG G in (3.1) is used to define dependencies between random variables $X^{0:N}$. It is also known as the structure of the BN. The vertex set V represents the set of random variables, while a directed edge $V_i \rightarrow V_j$ of the set of edges E represents a direct dependency between two variables. A missing edge symbolizes the independence of these two variables (cf. Figure 3.1).

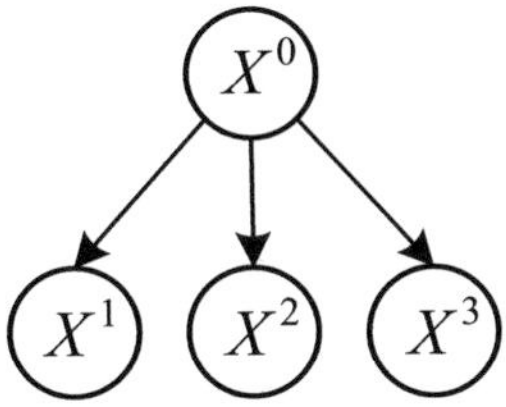

Figure 3.1: Graph of a Bayesian Network (BN) over random variables $X^{0:3}$. In this structure (also called Naive BN), there are directed edges connecting a root node (X^0) and its children ($X^{1:3}$). Since a missing edge symbolizes an independence of two variables, the joint probability $P(X^{0:3})$ can be factorized as follows: $P(X^{0:3}) = P(X^0)P(X^1|X^0)P(X^2|X^0)P(X^3|X^0)$.

The joint probability distribution in (3.2) is given by the product of all conditional probability distributions associated with the vertices of G. It is also known as the parameters of the BN. Here, $\text{Pa}(X^n)$ denotes the set of parents of a random variable X^n. Graphically, this corresponds to vertices having a directed edge pointing to X^n's vertex. Please note, if $\text{Pa}(X^n) = \emptyset$, a random variable X^n is a root node of the BN, and $P(X^n|\,\emptyset) = P(X^n)$ gives the a-priori probability (cf. Figure 3.1).

A Dynamic Bayesian Network (DBN) is an extension of a BN, also taking the temporal dependencies of variables into account [Mur02]. A DBN is given by a pair

$$DBN = (B_0, B_\rightarrow)\,,$$

where the BN B_0 uses $P(X_0^{0:N})$ to specify the a-priori probability distribution over random variables $X^{0:N}$ in a time step with index 0 (cf. Figure 3.1 as an example for a possible underlying DAG).

Furthermore, $B_\rightarrow$ specifies the conditional probability distribution over discrete time steps t by using

$$P(X_t^{0:N}|X_{t-1}^{0:N}) = \prod_{n=0}^{N} P(X_t^n|\text{Pa}(X_t^n))\,. \tag{3.3}$$

In Equation (3.3), $\text{Pa}(X_t^n)$ denotes the set of X_t^n's parents in the corresponding graph. The parents can be in the same time slice (e.g. representing instantaneous causation) or the previous one (i.e., we assume the model to be fist-order Markov). In the latter case, arcs point to time slices with ascending index, reflecting the causal flow of time [Mur02]. Please compare Figure 3.2 for an exemplary graph of $B_\rightarrow$ which is also known as a two-slice Temporal Bayesian Network (2TBN).

For T time-slices, the joint distribution of the DBN is given by equation [Mur02]:

$$\begin{aligned} P(X_{0:T}^{0:N}) &= \left(\prod_{n=0}^{N} P(X_0^n|\text{Pa}(X_0^n))\right) \prod_{t=1}^{T}\prod_{n=0}^{N} P(X_t^n|\text{Pa}(X_t^n)) \\ &= \prod_{t=0}^{T}\prod_{n=0}^{N} P(X_t^n|\text{Pa}(X_t^n))\,. \end{aligned}$$

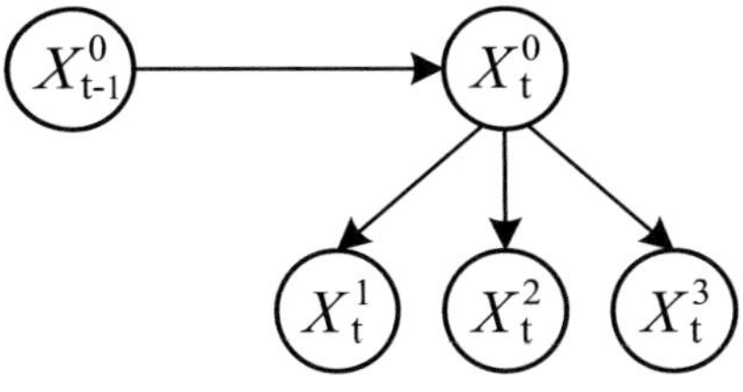

Figure 3.2: Simplified graph of a 2-Slice Temporal Bayesian Network (2TBN). In context of a DBN, a 2TBN (or: $B_{\rightarrow}$) is used as template for consecutive time steps t. For simplification, we omitted $X^{1:3}_{t-1}$, since in this example, there is no direct dependency to $X^{0:3}_t$.

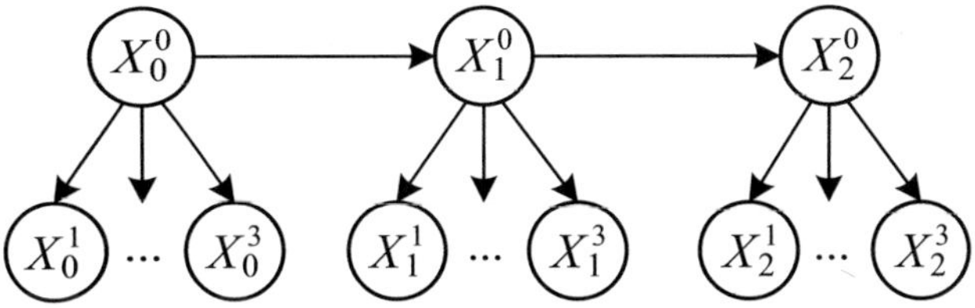

Figure 3.3: Example of a DBN unrolled for 3 slices using graphs depicted in Figure 3.1 and 3.2 as B_0 and $B_{\rightarrow}$. For simplification some nodes are omitted, which is graphically represented by three dots.

Graphically, this corresponds to an unrolling of the DBN, using B_0 as the initial distribution, and $B_{\rightarrow}$ as template for each following time slice. Refer to Figure 3.3 for a DBN unrolled for three time slices. Similar to HMMs, parameters of such a DBN, having N children, can be grouped as follows (cf. Figure 3.3):

$$P(X^0_0 = i) = \boldsymbol{\pi}(i) \tag{3.4}$$

$$P(X^0_t = j | X^0_{t-1} = i) = \boldsymbol{A}(i, j) \tag{3.5}$$

$$P(X^1_t = j | X^0_t = i) = \boldsymbol{B}^{(1)}(i, j) \tag{3.6}$$

$$\dots$$

$$P(X^N_t = j | X^0_t = i) = \boldsymbol{B}^{(N)}(i, j) \tag{3.7}$$

Equation (3.4) shows the inital probability distribution associated with the root node X^0 at time step $t = 0$ (X_0^0). Consequently, $\boldsymbol{\pi}(i)$ is a vector representing the a-priori probability of each of the values of X_0^0 being present. Please note that the statement $P(X = x)$ is a shorthand for an event $\omega \in \Omega : f_X(\omega) = x$, whereby the set of possible outcomes is denoted by Ω, and f_X maps an event ω to a possible value of a random variable X. We denote possible values x of X by $Val(X)$ [KF09].

In Equation (3.5) the probability distributions of the state transitions are given. With this, the dependencies over time (and between states) are expressed. Consequently, $\boldsymbol{A}(i, j)$ is an adjacency matrix extended by transition probabilities for entries unequal to 0. In Equations (3.6) and (3.7), the probability distribution for observations concerning the children of the root node are given. The naming of the matrices $\boldsymbol{A}(i, j)$ and $\boldsymbol{B}(i, j)$ is inspired by Hidden Markov Models (HMMs). Please note, that in case of HMMs the observation probabilities can be specified by a single matrix $\boldsymbol{B}(i, j)$, since the corresponding probability distribution cannot be factorized. That means, graphically, the root node would have only one child which incorporates the complete probability distribution.

4 Workflow of a Cholecystectomy

In Figure 4.1, the application example of this work, the workflow of a cholecystectomy (surgical removal of the gallbladder) is depicted.

The sequence of tasks is as follows: First, carbonic acid gas is injected to inflate the abdomen (stomach). In task two, trocars, sharpened tubes, are used to break through the abdominal wall. Trocars can be used to enable the placement of additional medical instruments during the surgery. In the third task of the workflow, the bile duct is dissected (exposed). The following task comprises the clipping and cutting of the bile duct. In task five the cystic artery is dissected in preparation for the clipping and cutting in task six. After this task, an intraoperative cholangiogram (radiographic imaging of the bile ducts with contrast medium) is optionally performed. Thus, a decision has to be made after task six. When the two possible flows are merged, another sequence of tasks has to be accomplished. It includes the detaching of the gallbladder and the liver bed coagulation.

Each of the tasks is represented by a set of characteristic features. In this work, we utilize surgical instruments to characterize the single tasks. The presence of a certain surgical instrument is given as observation for our phase detection models.

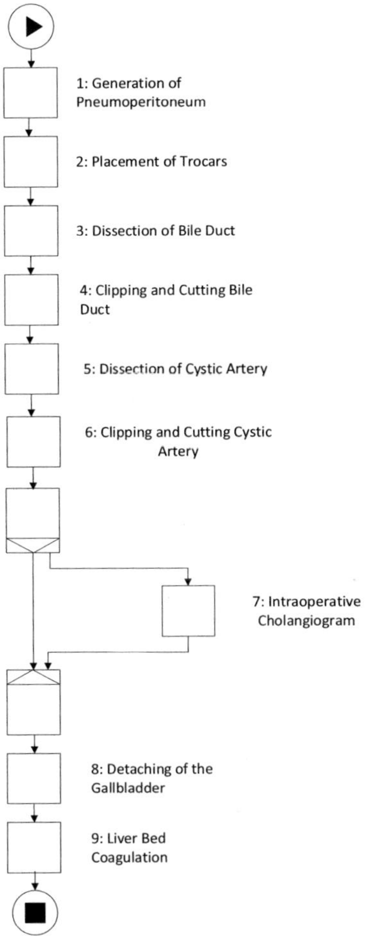

Figure 4.1: Workflow of a cholecystectomy (surgical removal of the gallbladder) in YAWL. A sequence of tasks is followed by a decision, and two additional tasks after the two possible flows are merged.

5 Combining YAWL and DBNs

To provide a reliable phase detection, we propose the combination of Yet Another Workflow Language (YAWL) with Dynamic Bayesian Networks (DBNs). YAWL is used to model the relationship between surgical phases, in the sense that possible transitions from one phase to another can be specified. The upper part of Figure 5.1 shows the YAWL model of an exemplary workflow with three subsequent phases a, b and c. The workflow starts with an input condition (black triangle in a circle) followed by the three tasks a, b, c (squares), and ends by a final condition (black square in a circle). A frame comprising the current phase and the subsequent phases is shifted while the workflow progresses. Depending on this frame, a different DBN model is chosen.

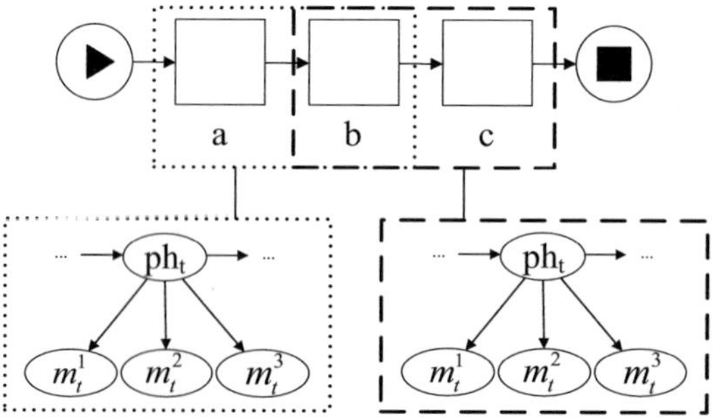

Figure 5.1: A combination of YAWL with DBNs is proposed in this work. YAWL symbols are depicted in the upper part of the figure. The workflow starts by an input condition (black triangle in a circle) followed by three tasks (squares) and ends by a final condition (black square in a circle). In the lower part of the figure, DBNs are shown. Each DBN is associated with a frame comprising the current task as well as possible follow up tasks.

In order to do so, the corresponding DBN models have to be linked with the state transitions of YAWL. In Figure 5.2 the internal structure of an atomic YAWL task is outlined. The notation is inspired by Petri Nets [Pet62], and assumes that there are so called transitions which consume marks, so-called tokens. Additionally, there are so called places where these tokens can be stored. Thereby, transitions can be interpreted as internal actions and places can be interpreted as internal states of a task t. The example in Figure 5.2 depicts a transition named *enter* which removes all tokens that enable the task t. In the simple case where task

t has no join behavior (e.g. there is only one predecessor task a before task b like in Fig. 5.1), there is only one token (resulting from the predecessor task) to remove respectively. If there is join behavior and $f_{\text{join}}(t) = \text{AND}$, all input places of the transition $enter_t$ need to hold a token. I.e., task t can only be entered iff all other predecessor tasks are exited. For $f_{\text{join}}(t) = \text{XOR}$ and $f_{\text{join}}(t) = \text{OR}$, different rules for joining apply. Here, at least one token has to be present. For more detailed information please refer to [AH03]. Further details on Petri Nets can be found in [Rei13b].

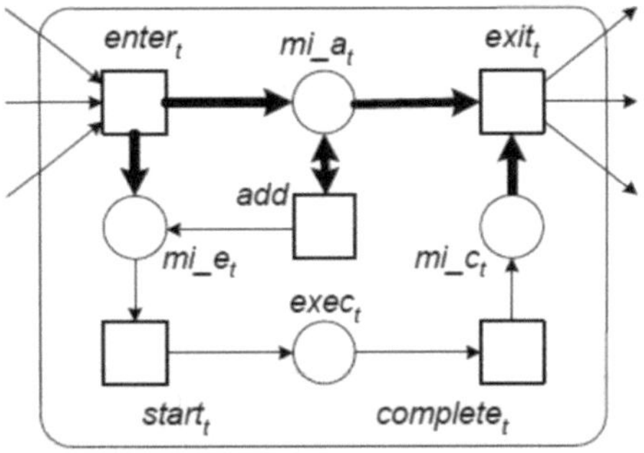

Figure 5.2: The internal states of an atomic YAWL task can be represented by a Petri Net inspired notation. Modified from [AH03].

In Figure 5.2, the places mi_a_t, mi_e_t, mi_c_t, and the transition *add* are necessary for managing multi-instance tasks. For simplification, we consider a task to be a single instance. That means one and the same task cannot be simultaneously executed more than once.

Once, the transition $enter_t$ has produced one token, the transition *start* is enabled and can occur. When the superordinate task t starts to be executed, the internal transition *start* consumes the corresponding token. While task t is executed, a token resides in place *exec*. As soon as the superordinate task t is completed, the transition *complete* consumes this token and produces a new token in the adjacent place. The tokens produced by transition *exit* can activate follow up tasks. Different activation mechanisms are possible: 1.) No split behavior, i.e., only one token allows to activate a subsequent task. 2.) In case of an AND-split, for each subsequent task, one token is produced. 3.) In case of XOR- or OR-split at least one token is produced for all of the successors.

In our approach that combines YAWL and DBNs, we chose the appropriate DBN model based on the current phase. The current phase is represented by the task currently executed, i.e., a token is present at the task's internal place *execute*. Each task is linked to a unique DBN model. This model consists of a root node containing the current task, as well as all follow-up tasks as possible outcomes. The follow-up tasks are given by the successors of the task's internal transition *exit*. All other tasks of the network are not considered for classification in this case. As soon as the DBN model predicts that a follow-up phase is present, the current YAWL task is exited and the predicted successor is executed. Once this happens, a new DBN model is activated and used for the following classification. The process can be described by sliding a classification window over the workflow (cf. Figure 5.1).

6 Verification

To verify our approach, we used expert-based modeled DBNs of a cholecystectomy [PFBss]. We generated 100 surgical procedures with simulated feature values, using a median of algorithmic accuracies of 92%. Out of the generated surgeries, 45 surgeries involved an intraoperative cholangiogram. The proposed combination of YAWL and DBNs was utilized to classify the generated observation sequences. Figure 6.1 depicts the resulting confusion matrix. The results show that the model is able to predict the correct task in most cases (overall accuracy of 89%). There is some confusion (which is expressed by the false classified off-diagonal elements, since they are mistakenly confused with other classes), especially in *Clipping and Cutting Cystic Artery* (task 6) and *Intraoperative Cholangiogram* (task 7). In the first case, the observations are predominantly confused with the two possible follow-up tasks (*Intraoperative Cholangiogram*, task 7, and *Detaching of the Gallbladder*, task 8). Further confusion is present in *Intraoperative Cholangiogram*, but predominantly with the last phase 9. This is, because the model can hardly compensate wrong predicted transitions, which is a direct consequence of the frame-wise moving classification window. To compensate this aspect, auxiliary backward transitions, e.g. to the previous task, could be added to the model. To sum up we can say that the proposed models work as expected. Nevertheless, there is room of improvement concerning the robustness of the classification which will be addressed in upcoming publications.

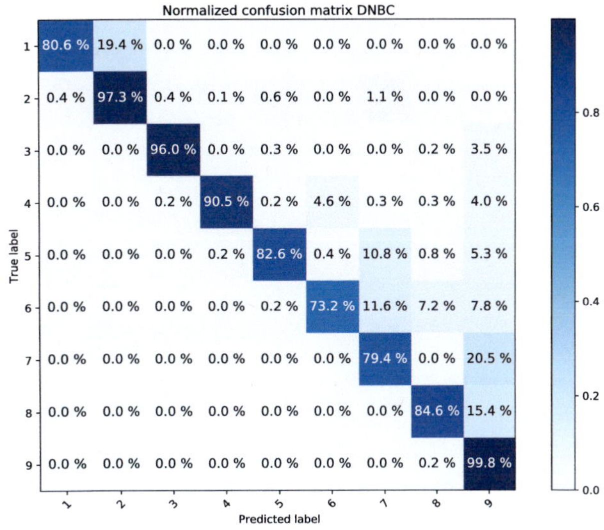

Figure 6.1: Normalized Confusion Matrix. A row represents an instance of an actual surgical step, whereas a column represents an instance of the predicted surgical step. Consequently, the values of the diagonal elements represent the degree of correctly predicted classes.

7 Conclusion

In this work, we discussed the fundamentals of YAWL (Yet Another Workflow Language) and DBNs (Dynamic Bayesian Networks) in detail. On that basis, we introduced a combination of YAWL and DBNs for a surgical phase detection on the application example of the removal of a gallbladder (cholecystectomy).

We showed that the proposed models are able to predict most of the tasks of the surgery correctly. Nevertheless, there is some room of improvement with respect to the robustness of the classification which will be adressed in future research.

Detecting the progress of an on-going surgery plays an important role for context sensitive assistance: A reliable detection of the current task of a surgical workflow is the basis for a tailored decision support for medical practitioners. Subsequently, an intraoperative support can help to prevent errors, injuries, negligence or malpractices.

Bibliography

[AH03] W Aalst and A Hofstede. Yawl: Yet another workflow language (revised version). Technical report, Technical Report FIT-TR-2003-04, Queensland University of Technology, Brisbane, 2003.

[DK89] Thomas Dean and Keiji Kanazawa. A model for reasoning about persistence and causation. *Computational intelligence*, 5(2):142–150, 1989.

[FL92] E Field and K Lohr. *Guidelines for Clinical Practice: From Development to Use*. National Academies Press, 1992.

[HRAA10] Arthur Hofstede, Nick Russell, Wil Aalst, and Michael Adams. *Modern Business Process Automation: YAWL and its Support Environment*. Springer, Berlin, 2010.

[KF09] Daphne Koller and Nir Friedman. *Probabilistic graphical models: principles and techniques*. MIT press, 2009.

[KWN$^+$15] HG Kenngott, M Wagner, F Nickel, AL Wekerle, A Preukschas, M Apitz, T Schulte, R Rempel, P Mietkowski, F Wagner, et al. Computer-assisted abdominal surgery: new technologies. *Langenbeck's Archives of Surgery*, 400(3):273–281, 2015.

[LJ14] Florent Lalys and Pierre Jannin. Surgical process modelling: a review. *International journal of computer assisted radiology and surgery*, 9(3):495–511, 2014.

[Mur02] Kevin Patrick Murphy. *Dynamic bayesian networks: representation, inference and learning*. PhD thesis, University of California, Berkeley, 2002.

[Pad10] Nicolas Padoy. *Workflow and Activity Modeling for Monitoring Surgical Procedures*. PhD thesis, Université Henri Poincaré-Nancy I, 2010.

[Pet62] Carl Adam Petri. *Kommunikation mit Automaten*. PhD thesis, Universität Bonn, 1962.

[PFBss] Patrick Philipp, Yvonne Fischer, and Jürgen Beyerer. Expert-based probabilistic modeling of workflows in context of surgical interventions. *CogSima 2017, IEEE Conference on Cognitive and Computational Aspects of Situation Management*, 2017, (in Press).

[PFHB16] Patrick Philipp, Yvonne Fischer, Dirk Hempel, and Jürgen Beyerer. Framework for an interactive assistance in diagnostic processes based on probabilistic modeling of clinical practice guidelines. In *Emerging Trends in Applications and Infrastructures for Computational Biology, Bioinformatics, and Systems Biology*, pages 371–390. Elsevier, 2016.

[Phi16] Patrick Philipp. Framework for modeling medical guidelines based on the translation of uml activities into yawl. Technical report, KIT Scientific Publishing, Karlsruhe, 2016.

[Rei13b] Wolfgang Reisig. *Understanding Petri Nets*. Springer, Heidelberg, 2013.

[SGM+11] Earl Steinberg, Sheldon Greenfield, Michelle Mancher, et al. *Clinical Practice Guidelines We Can Trust*. National Academies Press, 2011.

[VvdAtH06] HMW Verbeek, Wil MP van der Aalst, and Arthur HM ter Hofstede. Verifying workflows with cancellation regions and or-joins: an approach based on relaxed soundness and invariants. *The Computer Journal*, 50(3):294–314, 2006.

RNN-accelerated Experimental Design for Chromatic Confocal Measurement

Ding Luo

Vision and Fusion Laboratory
Institute for Anthropomatics
Karlsruhe Institute of Technology (KIT), Germany
ding.luo@kit.edu

Technical Report IES-2016-02

Abstract: With decades of research and development, confocal microscopes have been the work horse of scientific and industrial 3D measurement. However, due to its requirement for axial scanning, its range of application is limited by its slow measurement speed. Chromatic confocal measurement systems have been developed to eliminate the need for mechanical scanning. Nevertheless, they are still bottle-necked by the transfer and processing of densely sampled spectral data. In this article, Bayesian experimental design is applied to the chromatic confocal measurement scheme, allowing for more efficient spectral sampling. Recurrent neural network (RNN) is trained to approximate full Bayesian experimental design with much less computation. Simulations have demonstrated that experimental design approximated by RNN provides better results than an equidistant sampling scheme and performance close to full Bayesian experimental design.

1 Introduction

Confocal microscope has been widely applied in various fields due to its superior resolution and unique depth-discerning capability [HWS81]. In a conventional confocal system, a monochromatic point source is projected into the object space for illumination and the returning light is reflected to a pinhole which guarantees that light gets fully transmitted to the detector only when the object is in focus. In order to retrieve the depth information, the system has to

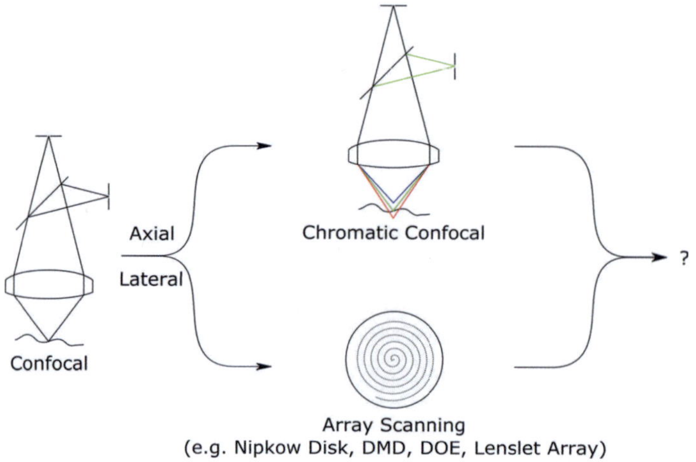

Figure 1.1: Confocal microscope requires both axial and lateral scanning.

be shifted axially with respect to the object while the detector records intensity measurements at different locations. This scanning generates a Gaussian-like signal which can be utilized to retrieve the depth of the object. In order to get a full 3D measurement of the object, the system has to be scanned also laterally. Confocal measurement is slow due to its requirement for axial and lateral scanning. Various technologies have been developed to accelerate these processes, such as chromatic confocal microscope [MPPQ84] and various array scanning microscopes [EAH02, DLY$^+$13]. However, two fundamental problems remain unsolved. In the axial direction, when we are dealing with confocal or chromatic confocal signal, we are always trying to locate the location of a quasi-Gaussian peak which directly reflects the location/depth of the object under measurement. According to estimation theory the width of the peak is directly related to the sensitivity of the system, and in this case people are always trying to build a system with a peak as narrow as possible in order to increase the sensitivity. Nevertheless, a narrower peak means that the information about the object is only contained within a tiny subset of support where all the rest of the signal are simply zeros. To measure the complete signal with such sparsity like what's typically done in a chromatic confocal system with spectrometer is highly inefficient. The second fundamental problem is related with the density of measurement. Light which is not focused on the object will spread across adjacent area of a single measurement point, limiting the minimum distance between two simultaneous lateral measurement points that prevents crosstalk. This article aims to tackle the first problem through simulations of Bayesian experimental design and its accelerated approximation based on Recurrent Neural Network.

2 Chromatic Confocal Measurement Model

The target of chromatic confocal measurement is to retrieve the depth of the measurement position via the location of the Gaussian-like peak. From the point of view of parameter estimation, the canonical way to do this is to build a measurement model and apply Bayesian inference on the parameters of interest. The measurement model is composed of two parts, the signal model and the noise model. The signal model describes the relationship between an ideal signal, or expectation of the signal, and the parameters to be estimated. And the noise model represents the amount of noise added to the ideal model.

In the case of chromatic confocal measurement, we assume that the signal is a Gaussian function expressed by the following equation:

$$\hat{y} = \theta_1 e^{-\frac{(\lambda-\theta_2)^2}{2\sigma^2}}$$

where θ_1 represents the amplitude of the signal and θ_2 represents the location of the signal. θ_1 is mainly determined by the reflectance of the object and θ_2 reflects the axial position of the object. λ denotes the wavelength. σ represents the width of the Gaussian-shaped chromatic confocal signal and is determined by properties of the optical system such as the numerical aperture. Assuming normally distributed noise, the complete model is expressed as a normal distribution over the combination of signal and noise:

$$y \sim \mathcal{N}(\hat{y}, \sigma_n) \tag{2.1}$$

where σ_n describes the variance of the noise and is mainly determined by the camera.

Based on Bayes theorem, the parameter estimation task is relatively straightforward by calculating the posterior probability distribution of the parameters based on the measurement model. In this case, the parameters of interest are

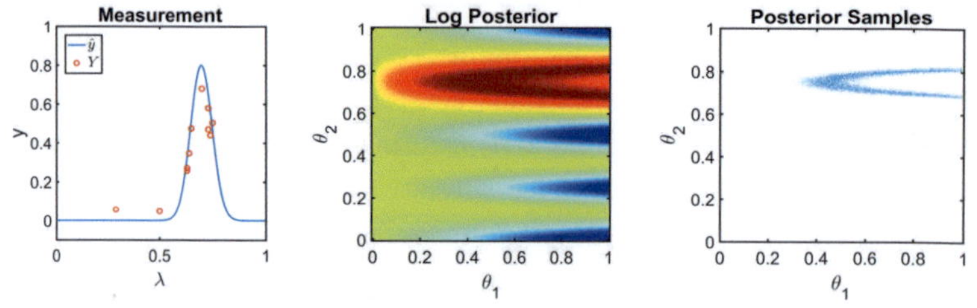

Figure 2.1: Posterior sampling after measurements are made.

$\boldsymbol{\theta} = \{\theta_1, \theta_2\}$, where θ_1 contains information of the object texture and θ_2 contains the depth information. The posterior is proportional to the product of prior and likelihood. Without any prior knowledge, the prior distribution is considered to be flat across the valid support so that all parameter values are equally possible when no measurements are made. The likelihood comes directly from the measurement model, as shown in Eq. (2.1). Therefore, the posterior distribution can be calculated up to a certain scale factor:

$$\begin{aligned} p(\boldsymbol{\theta}|y) &= \frac{p(\boldsymbol{\theta})p(y|\boldsymbol{\theta})}{p(y)} \\ &\propto p(\boldsymbol{\theta})p(y|\boldsymbol{\theta}) \end{aligned}$$

In practice, calculating the posterior distribution with certain resolution is often computationally prohibitive, and therefore people have been using sampling techniques such as Markov-Chain Monte Carlo (MCMC) method. In our case, an ensemble sampler which is affine-invariant [GW] is utilized for drawing the posterior samples. Once samples are drawn from the posterior distribution, the estimation becomes trivial by calculating the average of all samples.

Figure 2.1 demonstrates the procedure of posterior sampling for chromatic measurement through simulation. In the left figure, the signal to be measured is denoted by $\hat{y}$ and simulated measurements with normally distributed noise are contained in Y . The middle figure illustrates the posterior probability distribution of the parameters to be estimated and the right figure shows samples drawn from such distribution.

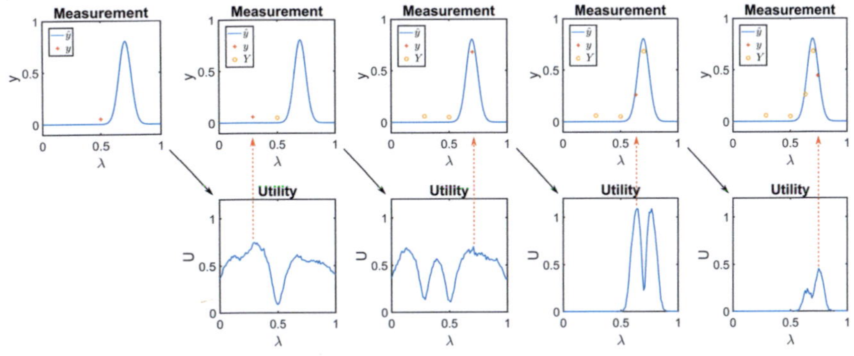

Figure 3.1: Adaptive measurement of a chromatic confocal signal. First row: each measurement step. Second row: utility function after each measurement step.

The Bayesian framework has two major advantages for parameter estimation. Firstly, the uncertainty of the estimation can be easily derived by calculating the variance of the samples. Secondly, the posterior distribution of the parameter allows for the selection of optimal measurement location in the next measurement through Bayesian experimental design, as will be discussed in the next section.

3 Bayesian Experimental Design

Bayesian experimental design is the subject of making decisions under uncertainties with limited resource. In our case of measuring a chromatic confocal signal, conventional systems utilize a spectrometer which disperse various wavelength onto hundreds of pixels. A major drawback for such approach is that the transfer of the intensity data can be quite slow. Additionally, in the case of multi-point chromatic confocal system, the application of multiple spectrometers is often prohibitive, due to either cost or mechanical constrains. Therefore, wavelength scanning of the light source is used instead to acquire the chromatic signal. Nevertheless, such process can be time-intensive depending on the scanning speed of the light source.

Instead of an equidistant measuring scheme, Bayesian experimental design allows for an adaptive measuring scheme, where location for new measurement is determined by measurements already conducted. For example, With a tunable light source whose wavelength can be tuned programmably, suppose that we have measured intensities of five wavelengths, the question that Bayesian experimental design tries to answer is which wavelength we should look at next so that estimation could be made most efficiently in the end.

The profit generated by measurement at a certain wavelength is described by a utility function over the design space. There are various different utility functions which focuses on different aspects of the design. Here we will take the Kullback-Leibler divergence between the posterior and the new posterior with the new measurement. The utility function is expressed as the expectation of this KL divergence under the posterior predictive distribution [Rya03]:

$$
\begin{aligned}
U(d) &= \mathbb{E}_{y|d}[D_{\mathrm{KL}}(p(\boldsymbol{\theta}|Y, y, d) \| p(\boldsymbol{\theta}|Y))] \\
&= \iint p(\boldsymbol{\theta}|Y, y, d) \log \frac{p(\boldsymbol{\theta}|Y, y, d)}{p(\boldsymbol{\theta}|Y)} \mathrm{d}\boldsymbol{\theta} p(y|Y, d) \mathrm{d}y \\
&= \iint p(\boldsymbol{\theta}|Y) p(y|\boldsymbol{\theta}, d) \big[\log p(y|\boldsymbol{\theta}, Y, d) \\
&\quad - \log[\int p(\boldsymbol{\theta}|Y, d) p(y|\boldsymbol{\theta}, Y, d) \mathrm{d}\boldsymbol{\theta}] \big] \mathrm{d}\boldsymbol{\theta} \mathrm{d}y \\
&\approx \frac{1}{N} \sum_{i=1}^{N} \Big\{ \log p(y^i|\boldsymbol{\theta}^i, d) - \log \big[\frac{1}{M} \sum_{j=1}^{M} p(y^i|\boldsymbol{\theta}^{ij}, d) \big] \Big\} \\
&\quad \{\boldsymbol{\theta}^i\} \cup \{\boldsymbol{\theta}^{ij}\} \sim p(\boldsymbol{\theta}|Y), \{y^i\} \sim p(y|\boldsymbol{\theta}^i, d)
\end{aligned}
$$

where d represents possible design, i.e. next wavelength to be measured. Calculation of the double integral for this utility function cannot be conducted analytically and therefore is solved by a nested Monte Carlo approximation using posterior samples drawn for parameter estimation.

Finally, the task is to find the d^* which maximizes the utility function above. Although there are stochastic optimization techniques for such problems, people typically calculate the utility functions for a grid of design points and take the maximum one. Notice that this approach is based on the so-called myopic design. It means that only one further step is considered based on current situation. This does not guarantee true optimal design for an experiment with multiple measurements, but in general works very well as a greedy method.

As an example, Figure 3.1 demonstrates the adaptive measurement of a chromatic confocal signal. The first row shows the signal to be measured and the corresponding measurement in each step. In these graphs, $\hat{y}$ denotes the signal to be measured, y represents new measurement in each step and Y contains all measurements conducted. The second row shows the utility function over the design space in each step. In this example, measurement starts by recording intensity of the wavelength in the middle. Based on the measurement result, parameter estimation is conducted and the utility function over all wavelengths is calculated. In the next step, intensity is measured at the wavelength which has the largest utility value.These two steps can be repeated multiple times until utility functions for all positions drops to zero, indicating that new measurements do not bring any additional information. The wavelength is normalized to a range from zero to one as the calculations are all based on simulations.

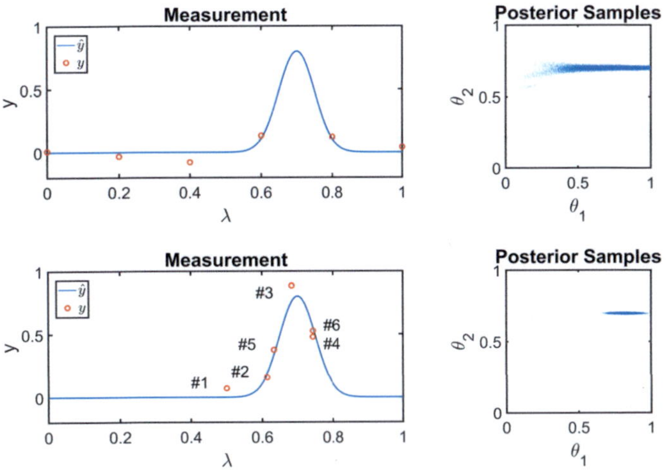

Figure 3.2: Comparison between equidistant measurement and adaptive measurement. First row: equidistant measurement and its corresponding posterior estimation. Second row: adaptive measurement and its corresponding posterior estimation.

Figure 3.2 shows the comparison between equidistant measurement scheme and adaptive measurement scheme based on Bayesian experimental design. As seen from the posterior samples, with same number of measurement steps, the adaptive approach typically generates much concentrated samples, indicating less uncertainty for parameter estimation. The reason is that the adaptive approach tends to make new measurements at locations where more information is expected to be gained about the parameters.

4 Accelerated Experimental Design with RNN

As discussed in Section 3, the utility function in Bayesian experimental design can be approximated by a nested Monte Carlo method:

$$U(d) \approx \hat{U}_{N,M} \equiv \frac{1}{N}\sum_{i=1}^{N}\Big\{\log p(y^i|\boldsymbol{\theta}^i,d) - \log\big[\frac{1}{M}\sum_{j=1}^{M} p(y^i|\boldsymbol{\theta}^{ij},d)\big]\Big\}$$

where $\{\boldsymbol{\theta}^i\} \cup \{\boldsymbol{\theta}^{ij}\}$ are drawn from $p(\boldsymbol{\theta}|Y)$ and $\{y^i\}$ are drawn from $p(y|\boldsymbol{\theta}^i, d)$.

One major disadvantage of Bayesian experimental design is its slow speed. The nested MC approximation of the utility function shown above is only asymptotically unbiased as an estimator of the utility function. The bias and variance of estimator depends on the number of posterior samples. As shown in previous study [Rya03], the variance can be represented as $A(d)/N + B(d)/NM$ and the bias can be represented to leading order by $C(d)/M$, where A, B and C are terms depending on the sampling distribution. The number of samples needed for experimental design is naturally much larger than that for inference. To make things even worse, the inner loop of this nested MC is performed for each design candidate respectively. Due to these reasons, even with faster computers nowadays, full Bayesian experimental design is only implemented in limited fields, such as pharmaceutical studies and astronomy. What's common about these fields is that although the model behind is often very complex, the time interval between two experiments are also very long, thus allowing a good design to be found in a Bayesian way.

The problem of measuring the chromatic confocal signal is exactly opposite. Real-time decisions have to be made based on a relatively simple model. If the design speed is not fast enough, it would be more efficient to simply scan the whole wavelength range like a spectrometer. To accelerate the Bayesian experimental design process, a specific type of neural network, i.e. recurrent neural network (RNN) can be trained as an approximation.

The inspiration for using this model originates from a recent topic in computer vison society, called Visual Attention Model [BMK14]. For pattern recognition

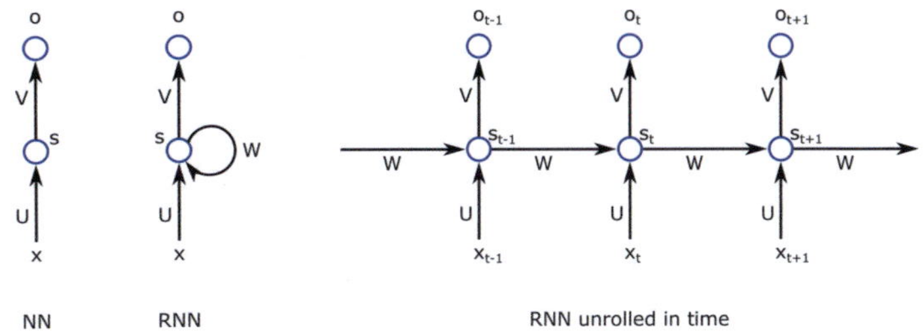

Figure 4.1: Graph representations of feed-forward neural network and recurrent neural network.

task, the researchers try to mimic the human vision system using a recurrent network. Instead of performing classification on the complete image, a small image patch is processed by the RNN and the output is both the classification result and where to look next. The training is implemented with reinforcement learning. It seems quite obvious that the visual attention model and Bayesian experimental design share an incredible amount of similarities as both attempt to gain more information through a series of adaptive measurements/observations.

For a conventional feed-forward neural network with a single hidden layer, the propagation of data can be expressed as:

$$s = f_1(Ux + b_1)$$
$$o = f_2(Vs + b_2)$$

where x denotes the input signal, o and s represent the activation of the hidden layer and the output layer respectively. The matrices U and V contain weights describing connections between layers. The non-linear activation functions with various choices are labeled as $f_1(\cdot)$ and $f_2(\cdot)$ with b_1 and b_2 representing biases. More layers can be added to form more complex networks.

A recurrent neural network is capable of "memorizing" previous input data due to the introduction of a feedback loop in the hidden layer. Although more sophisticated variations have been developed, the simplest form of a RNN can be expressed as:

$$s_t = f_1(Ux_t + Ws_{t-1} + b_1)$$
$$o_t = f_2(Vs_t + b_2)$$

where t stands for the time-stamp and W is a matrix describing the weights of the feedback loop.

To train a RNN for approximation of Bayesian experimental design, a series of experiments are simulated based on the measurement model and full Bayesian experimental design. Each simulated experiment consists of ten measurement steps of one chromatic confocal peak. The measurements and the corresponding utility functions are stored as training data for the RNN, which can be expressed in the following form:

$$\begin{aligned} l_t &= U\lambda_t + b_l \\ m_t &= Vi_t + b_m \\ s_t &= l_t \circ m_t \\ k_t &= LSTM(W, s_t, s_{t-1}, b_k) \\ o_t &= ReLU(Ok_t + b_o) \end{aligned}$$

where l_t is a hidden layer with 200 neurons to encode the measurement location, m_t is a hidden layer also with 200 neurons to encode the measured intensity. s_t merges l_t and m_t by taking element-wise multiplication with the Hadamard operator denoted by $\circ$. k_t is a sophisticated recurrent layer, namely Long Short-Term Memory (LSTM) [HS97], which memorizes information from previous measurement steps of an experiment. o_t is the output layer with rectified linear unit (ReLU) as the activation function. U, V, W, O contains weights describing each layer and b_l, b_m, b_k, b_o describe biases for the corresponding layers. The target of training is to find the weights and biases which best fit the simulated experiments and the training is conducted through RMSProp optimizer with the objective of minimizing the mean squared logarithmic error. The whole process is implemented in Python based on Theano and Keras, and is computed using Quadro K1100M graphics card by Nvidia. The training takes a couple of hours, but during measurement, the feed-forward calculation of a RNN is much faster than full Bayesian experimental design which requires multiple nested MC samplings.

As a comparison, 300 experiments of chromatic confocal measurements are simulated using three approaches: full Bayesian experimental design, approximation using RNN, and equidistant measurement. Parameters of the signal are drawn randomly. As can be seen from Figure 4.2, measurement with Bayesian experimental design has a lower average estimation bias compared with an equidistant measurement method when the number of measurements are equal. The approximation by recurrent neural network does not perform as well as the Bayesian experimental design, due to the errors generated in the utility functions. However, it still yields lower bias for parameter estimation compared with the equidistant measurement scheme.

Conventional feed-forward neural network with even just a single hidden layer, is proven to be a universal approximator [Cyb89]. It means that any function can be approximated by a neural network with a single hidden layer as long as the layer is large enough. RNN is even better and has been proven to be Turing-complete [Sie95]. While training of feed-forward neural network can be seen as optimization over functions, training of recurrent neural network can be seen as optimization over programs. There exists theoretically one RNN which perfectly approximates Bayesian experimental design of a specific model.

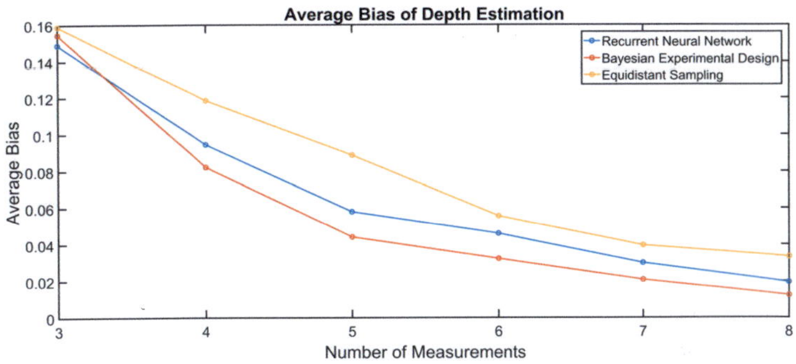

Figure 4.2: Comparison of different measurement schemes.

5 Conclusion

In this article, Bayesian experimental design is applied to chromatic confocal measurement technology in order to accelerate the measurement process through an adaptive procedure. Simulations based on Markov-Chain Monte Carlo sampling are conducted to calculate the expected Kullback-Leibler divergence of the posterior distribution after a new measurement step, which serves as the utility function for guiding the next measurement step. Although experiments conducted through Bayesian experimental design demonstrate better parameter inference accuracy than common equidistant measurement schemes, the computation for the nested MC approximation of the utility function is very intensive. Therefore, a recurrent neural network based on LSTM is trained in order to approximate full Bayesian experimental design with much faster speed. Simulations have shown that accelerated experimental design with RNN provides better results than an equidistant sampling scheme and performance close to full Bayesian experimental design.

All results presented in this report are derived from simulations based on an ideal measurement model with Gaussian-shaped confocal signal. Although widely accepted, such Gaussian signal model might not truly reflect practical situations, where the confocal peak can be asymmetric depending on the specific optical setup. Therefore, a more accurate measurement model should be built based on the actual hardware implementation. Real measurements based on Bayesian experimental design should be recorded to serve as the training data for the RNN to get a more valid approximation.

Bibliography

[BMK14] J. Ba, V. Mnih, and K. Kavukcuoglu. Multiple object recognition with visual attention. *CoRR*, abs/1412.7755, 2014.

[Cyb89] G. Cybenko. Approximation by superpositions of a sigmoidal function. *Mathematics of Control, Signals and Systems*, 2(4):303–314, 1989.

[DLY+13] D. Dan, M. Lei, B. Yao, W. Wang, M. Winterhalder, A. Zumbusch, Y. Qi, L. Xia, S. Yan, Y. Yang, P. Gao, T. Ye, and W. Zhao. DMD-based LED-illumination Super-resolution and optical sectioning microscopy. *Scientific Reports*, 3:1116, January 2013.

[EAH02] A. Egner, V. Andresen, and S. W. Hell. Comparison of the axial resolution of practical nipkow-disk confocal fluorescence microscopy with that of multifocal multiphoton microscopy: theory and experiment. *Journal of Microscopy*, 206(1):24–32, 2002.

[GW] J. Goodman and J. Weare. Ensemble samplers with affine invariance. *Communications in applied mathematics and computational science*, 5(1):65–80.

[HS97] S. Hochreiter and J. Schmidhuber. Long short-term memory. *Neural Computation*, 9(8):1735–1780, Nov 1997.

[HWS81] D. K. Hamilton, T. Wilson, and C. J. R. Sheppard. Experimental observations of the depth-discrimination properties of scanning microscopes. *Opt. Lett.*, 6(12):625–626, Dec 1981.

[MPPQ84] G. Molesini, G. Pedrini, P. Poggi, and F. Quercioli. Focus-wavelength encoded optical profilometer. *Optics Communications*, 49(4):229 – 233, 1984.

[Rya03] K. J. Ryan. Estimating expected information gains for experimental designs with application to the random fatigue-limit model. *Journal of Computational and Graphical Statistics*, 12(3):585–603, 2003.

[Sie95] H. T. Siegelmann. Computation beyond the turing limit. *Science*, 268(5210):545–548, 1995.

Anomaly detection using the Nash equilibrium in a multi-agent system

Mathias Anneken

Vision and Fusion Laboratory
Institute for Anthropomatics
Karlsruhe Institute of Technology (KIT), Germany
mathias.anneken@kit.edu

Technical Report IES-2016-03

Abstract: In order to support operators of surveillance systems and to improve their situation awareness, the automatic detection of unusual behavior and anomalies can provide an essential contribution. As the amount of available data increases due to cheaper and more proficient sensor systems like video cameras and radar systems, a human operator might not be able to cope with it. This might result in a misinterpreted situation and ultimately in making wrong decisions. Therefore, this report deals with an anomaly detection algorithm based on a multi-agent system. Each object in the monitored area is modeled as an agent with its own utility function. The agents are supposed to behave in a rational way. As the Nash equilibrium is a game theoretic concept to utilize rational behavior, the approach in this report is to use this solution concept to model the agents' behavior.

1 Introduction

In surveillance tasks, the automatic analysis of behavior is crucial to improve the situation awareness of operators. Fischer and Beyerer stated in [FB13], that the biggest challenge in advanced surveillance systems is not the acquisition of the data, but the processing of the data. With the increasing amount of available data, a human can be overwhelmed and needs support in order to be able to extract the relevant information from the data.

An idea to support an operator is the usage of situation analysis and anomaly detection tools. In [FRB14], Fischer et al. use an approach based on dynamic Bayesian network in order to model specific situations. By analyzing incoming data, the probability for the existence of the situation can be estimated. It is possible to build an abstract situation like smuggling goods or a pirate attack by evaluating the probabilities of elementary situations like an object is approaching another object, or the speed of an object is suspicious. The dynamic Bayesian network is more robust to outliers than a model based on logical expressions and rules alone.

Another approach is given in [AFB16]. Anneken et al. present an anomaly detection algorithm based on b-splines. The spatio-temporal data recorded in a surveillance task is interpolated by using splines. The resulting control points are then used as feature vector for machine learning algorithms. These are trained and used for the anomaly detection.

2 Intelligent Agent

An agent is defined by Russell and Norvig [RN95] as an object, which can use sensors to perceive the environment and effectors to interact with it. E.g., a human has its five senses as sensors and hands and legs as effectors. An intelligent agent reacts on the perceived environment in a specific way by evaluating the input and reasoning about possible actions. For Russell and Norvig, there are several levels of intelligence in agents. First, an agent can react with simple reflexes to the environment, i.e. the agent has stored some kind of rule base and reacts according to it. The more intelligent agents have goals they follow and utilities they can gain by performing an action. The most intelligent agent in this concept is a learning agent. This is an agent, which not only reacts but can learn new behavior in order to maximize its utility. In this report, the concept of an utility-based agent is used.

A utility-based agent as shown in Fig. 2.1 perceives its environment and derives its own state and the world's state from this information. It knows its possible actions and can estimate the state of the world, after performing a specific action. As the goals of the agent are given as its utility function, the agent is able to deduce its reward for each action. Therefore, the agent can choose the action with the highest utility and behave according to this strategy.

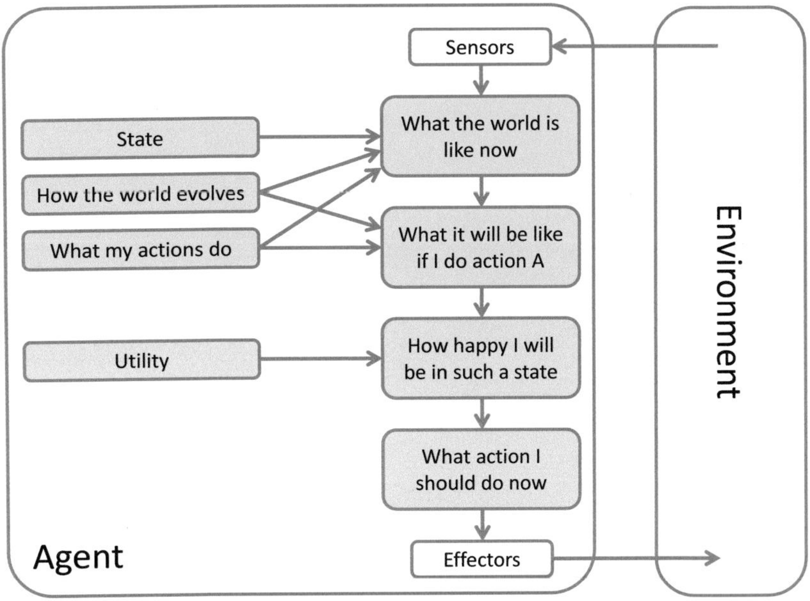

Figure 2.1: Structure of an utility-based agent as shown in [RN95].

One possible method to model a surveillance task with a multi-agent system is, to design for each object in the monitored area an agent. These agents have goals of their own, like following a specific trajectory or reaching a destination. The possible strategies are given by the utilized motion model in combination with the perceived environment. Following Anneken et al. [AFB17], the state of the agent i at a timestep t is given by its position $p_{t,i} = (p_{x_{t,i}}, p_{y_{t,i}})$, its moving direction $\phi_{t,i}$ and its speed $v_{t,i}$, resulting in

$$x_{t,i} = (p_{x_{t,i}}, p_{y_{t,i}}, \phi_{t,i}, v_{t,i})^\mathsf{T}$$

A simple motion model may consist of the change in direction $\delta_{\phi,i}$ and speed $\delta_{v,i}$. For a given maximum speed $v_{i,\max}$ and maximum turning angle in each timestep $\phi_{i,\max}$, these variables are defined by $\delta_{v,i} \in [-v_{i,\max}, v_{i,\max}]$ and the change of the heading $\delta_{\phi,i} \in [-\phi_{i,\max}, \phi_{i,\max}]$. The speed and direction of movement for the next timestep $t + 1$ is then defined as

$$\begin{aligned} v_{t+1,i} &= \delta_{v,i} \\ \phi_{t+1,i} &= \phi_{t,i} + \delta_{\phi,i}. \end{aligned}$$

The position is estimated by calculating the distance covered by the agent in the direction of $\phi_{t+1,i}$ with the speed $v_{t+1,i}$:

$$\begin{aligned} p_{x_{t+1,i}} &= p_{x_{t,i}} + v_{t+1,i} \cos(\phi_{t+1,i}) \\ p_{y_{t+1,i}} &= p_{y_{t,i}} + v_{t+1,i} \sin(\phi_{t+1,i}). \end{aligned}$$

The goals of the agents are defined as utility functions. For this report, three functions are implemented: one to arrive at a destination, one to follow a route, and one to keep distance to other agents. The mean value of the functions matches the utility for an agent.

The first function, reaching the destination $p_{i,d}$, is implemented as the ratio between the distance to the destination at the timestep $t+1$ and the distance to the destination at the timestep t

$$u_d = \frac{\|p_{t+1,i} - p_{i,d}\|}{\|p_{t,i} - p_{i,d}\|}.$$

The symbol $\|\cdot\|$ denotes the euclidean norm. In Fig. 2.2, the utility function is shown as a gradient from black (low utility value) to white (high utility value).

The utility function, which rewards following a route, is given by the euclidean distance $d_{r,i}$ between the route and $p_{t+1,i}$. As not all agents might want to stay in the same proximity of its route, this behavior can be modified by the parameter d_r. This results in the following utility function

$$u_r = \begin{cases} 1, & \text{if } d_{r,i} \leq d_r \\ -\frac{1}{d_r} \cdot d_{r,i} + 2, & \text{otherwise} \end{cases},$$

which is shown in Fig. 2.3.

The utility for a player i for keeping distance to other players is given by

$$u_p = \min_{j \in N \setminus \{i\}} \left(\min \left(\frac{\|p_{t+1,i}, p_{t+1,j}\|}{d_p}, 1 \right) \right).$$

The parameter d_p is used to adjust the distance, a player likes to keep to the other players. The utility function is depicted in Fig. 2.4.

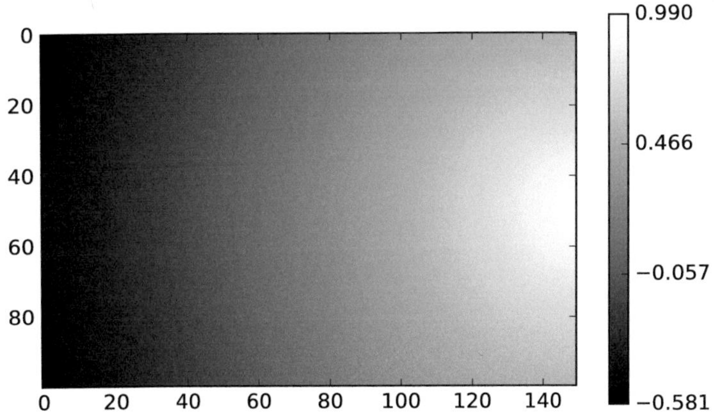

Figure 2.2: u_d for a player at $(50, 50)$ on the route $(0, 50) \rightarrow (150, 50)$. The gradient from black to white represent the utility of the player.

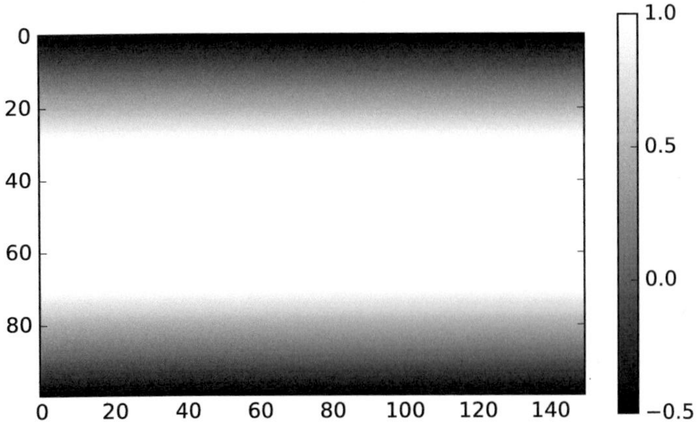

Figure 2.3: u_r for a player at $(50, 50)$ going on the route $(0, 50) \rightarrow (150, 50)$ and $d_r = 20$. The gradient from black to white represent the utility of the player.

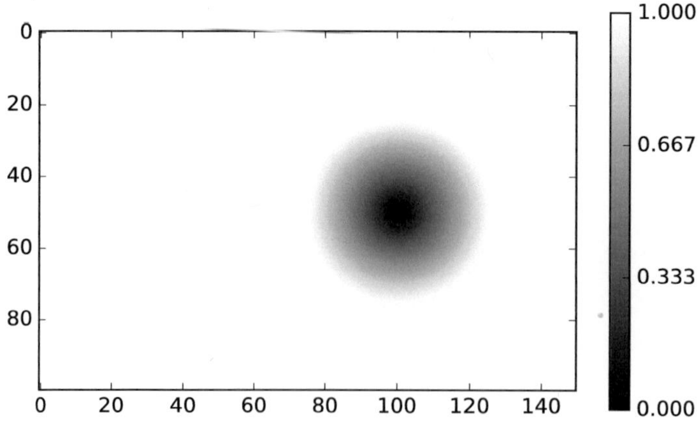

Figure 2.4: u_p for a player at $(50, 50)$ and a stationary player at $(100, 50)$ and $d_p = 25$. The gradient from black to white represent the utility of the player.

3 Nash Equilibrium

A game is denoted by Γ and defined as

$$\Gamma = (N, S, u),$$

with the set of player $N \subseteq \mathbb{N}$, the strategy space S and the payoff or reward function $u \in \mathbb{R}^n$. Each player i involved in the game Γ is in the set $N = \{1, \ldots, n\}$. The number of players $n \in \mathbb{N}$ is defined as $|N| = n$. A player can not only be a human being, but although an inanimate object or a group of objects. In case of a group, the whole group has to act as one and pursue the same goal.

The strategy space S contains all valid strategy combinations of the players. Each player $i \in N$ with $m \in \mathbb{N}$ possible strategies has its own strategy space S_i. A strategy for i is denoted by $s_i \in S_i$. The set of possible strategy combinations is then given by $S = S_1 \times \cdots \times S_n$. The strategy space for the players $N \setminus \{i\}$ is given by S_{-i} and a specific strategy combination for these players is given by $s_{-i} \in S_{-i}$. A strategy combination $s \in S$ can then be written as $s = (s_i, s_{-i})$.

This denotes a combination of a specific strategy s_i of player i and a strategy combination of all other players s_{-i}.

In a game, each player decides to follow a feasible strategy. Many games consist of several turns for each player. Therefore, the players have to choose a strategy in each of their turns. If a player has to choose exactly one strategy, it is a pure strategy. If probability is assigned to the strategies, it is called a mixed strategy.

The function, that assigns a specific payoff to all players in N for all of the strategy combinations S is called a payoff function, given by $u : S \to \mathbb{R}^n$. The payoff for an individual player $i \in N$ is given by the utility function $u_i : S \to \mathbb{R}$. The whole payoff vector is denoted by $u = (u_1, \dots, u_i, \dots, u_n)^\mathsf{T}$.

A strategy $s_i^* \in S_i$ for a player i is called dominant, if there is no other strategy $s_i \in S_i \setminus \{s_i^*\}$ with a higher payoff:

$$u_i(s_i^*, s_{-i}) > u_i(s_i, s_{-i}) \quad \forall s_{-i} \in S_{-i}, \forall s_i \in S_i \setminus \{s_i^*\}$$

A weak dominance is given by

$$u_i(s_i^*, s_{-i}) \geq u_i(s_i, s_{-i}) \quad \forall s_{-i} \in S_{-i}, \forall s_i \in S_i \setminus \{s_i^*\}$$

and for at least one strategy $s = (s_i, s_{-i})$

$$u_i(s_i^*, s_{-i}) > u_i(s_i, s_{-i})$$

holds true.

As the players are supposed to behave rational, they will never choose a dominated strategy. If a dominant strategy for a player i exists, the player will always choose this strategy, because all the other solutions will yield a lower payoff. An equilibrium in dominant strategies is given, if each player chooses its dominant strategy s_i^*.

An example for this solution concept is the prisoner's dilemma as given in Fig. 3.1. In this standard example, two members of a criminal organization are arrested. The prisoners cannot communicate with each other. The prosecutor has not enough evidence to convict the criminals for all their crimes, but only for a minor crime. Therefore, both prisoners will serve 2 years, if both of them remain silent (s_{11} and s_{21}). The prosecutor offers both criminals a bargain: if they testify, that the other has done the major crime, they will serve only 1 year in prison and the other will serve 10 years (either the combination s_{12} and s_{21}, or s_{11} and s_{22}). If both testify, they will serve 8 years in prison (s_{12} and s_{22}). In this game, the strategy to testify is dominant: If one of the criminals chooses to remain silent, the optimal strategy for the other player will be to testify. Thus, both criminals will serve 8 years in prison.

	s_{21}	s_{22}
s_{11}	$(-2, -2)$	$(-10, -1)$
s_{12}	$(-1, -10)$	$(-8, -8)$

Figure 3.1: Payoff matrix for the prisoner's dilemma.

A flaw for this solution concept is, that there are not always dominant strategies in a game. Therefore, Nash has developed another solution concept in [Nas50], the Nash equilibrium. It is defined as a strategy $s_i^* \in S_i$, which a player will choose as optimal strategy given that all other players will choose their optimal strategy. There is no incentive for a player to deviate from their optimal strategy.

$$u_i(s_i^*, s_{-i}^*) \geq u_i(s_i, s_{-i}^*) \quad \forall i \in N, \forall s_i \in S_i$$

4 Example

The results for an example game are given in Fig. 4.1 and Fig. 4.2. The game consists of two players with $v_{\text{max}} = 50$ and $\phi_{\text{max}} = \frac{\pi}{4}$. The first player follows the route $(300, 35) \rightarrow (0, 35)$ while the second player follows the route $(0, 25) \rightarrow (300, 25)$. In Fig. 4.1, the parameter d_p is varied. It can be seen, that by increasing d_p each player tries to keep a greater distance to each other.

In Fig. 4.2, only one timestep is shown. As the Nash equilibrium is ambiguous in this timestep, both strategies in the figure are possible directions for the objects. This problem can be solved, e.g., by preferring to pass another object on the right hand side, or by introducing other mechanisms.

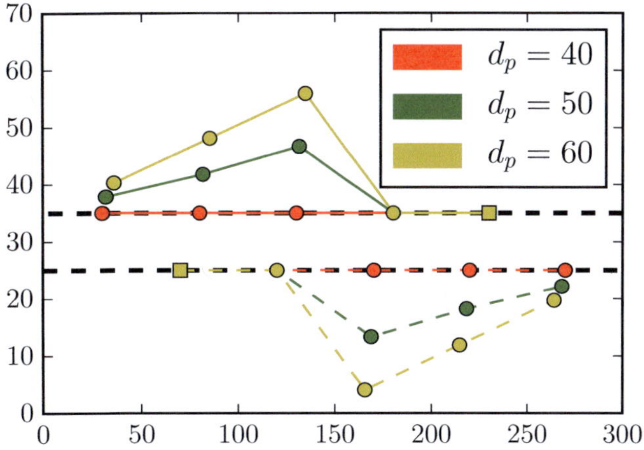

Figure 4.1: Example game. The dashed black lines represent the routes of the players. The stroked lines represent player one, the dashed lines player two. The parameter d_p is varied, in order to visualize its impact.

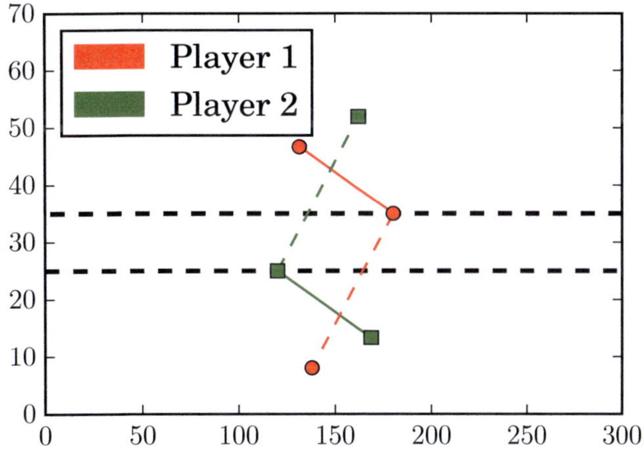

Figure 4.2: Ambiguous solutions for one timestep in the example game. For this timestep, two possible solutions exists. Either both try to pass the other object on its right hand side (dashed path) or on its left hand side (stroked path).

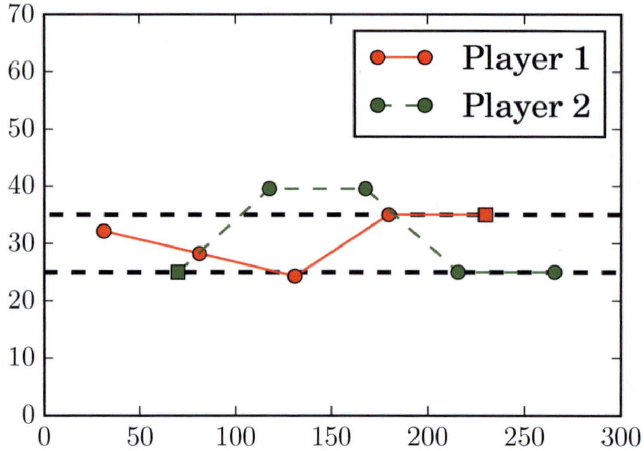

Figure 4.3: The starting position is the same as in Fig. 4.1. Player 1 behaves according to the Nash equilibrium, while player 2 behaves abnormal.

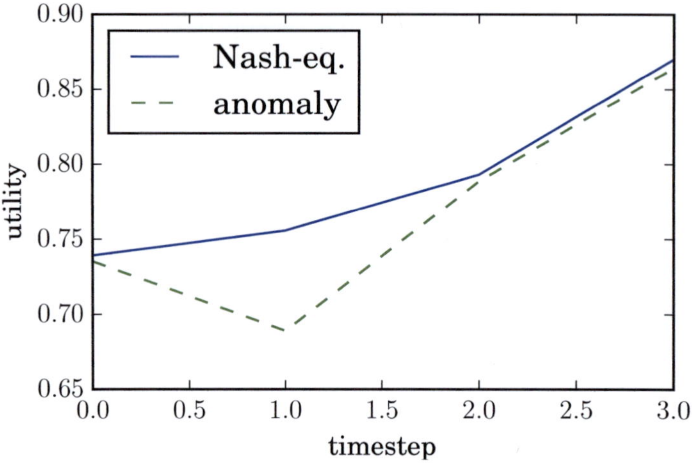

Figure 4.4: Comparison of the utility for player 2 in Fig. 4.3.

In Fig. 4.3, the first player behaves like the Nash equilibrium would suggest in each timestep. The second player behaves irrational. The paths each player takes are shown in the figure. The utility for each timestep for the second player is shown in Fig. 4.4. One line depicts the expected utility if the player would behave according to the Nash equilibrium. The other one shows the utility the player received by following the irrational behavior. The gained utility is always lower than the expected. The ratio between the actual achieved utility and the expected utility can be used to identify anomalies in the behavior of the agents.

5 Conclusion

In this report, a possible way to model a surveillance system using a multi-agent system is described. As one important task is the analysis of the behavior of objects in a monitored area, the decision process for a specific strategy is done by using the Nash equilibrium. It is shown, how this solution concept can be used to model the rational behavior of objects. Furthermore, the application of this behavior simulation for anomaly detection is shown.

Bibliography

[AFB16] Mathias Anneken, Yvonne Fischer, and Jürgen Beyerer. Anomaly detection using b-spline control points as feature space in annotated trajectory data from the maritime domain. In *Proceedings of the 8th International Conference on Agents and Artificial Intelligence*, volume 2, pages 250–257, 2016.

[AFB17] Mathias Anneken, Yvonne Fischer, and Jürgen Beyerer. A multi-agent approach to model and analyze the behavior of vessels in the maritime domain. In *Proceedings of the 9th International Conference on Agents and Artificial Intelligence - Volume 1: ICAART,*, pages 200–207, 2017.

[FB13] Y. Fischer and J. Beyerer. Ontologies for probabilistic situation assessment in the maritime domain. In *Cognitive Methods in Situation Awareness and Decision Support (CogSIMA), 2013 IEEE International Multi-Disciplinary Conference on*, pages 102–105, Feb 2013.

[FRB14] Y. Fischer, A. Reiswich, and J. Beyerer. Modeling and recognizing situations of interest in surveillance applications. In *Cognitive Methods in Situation Awareness and Decision Support (CogSIMA), 2014 IEEE International Inter-Disciplinary Conference on*, pages 209–215, March 2014.

[Nas50] John Forbes Nash. *Non-cooperative games*. PhD thesis, Princeton University, 1950.

[RN95] Stuart Russell and Peter Norvig. *Artificial Intelligence: A Modern Approach*. Prentice Hall, 1995.

Towards Surface Inference in Industrial Inspection

Mahsa Mohammadikaji

Vision and Fusion Laboratory
Institute for Anthropomatics
Karlsruhe Institute of Technology (KIT), Germany
mahsa.mohammadikaji@kit.edu

Technical Report IES-2016-04

Abstract: Automated product inspection play an important role in today's manufacturing process, and therefore, the design of optimized and precise measurement setups are a requirement for efficient product quality assurance. Due to the high dimensionality of the design space, a manual choice of the geometrical and optical parameters is associated with high costs, tedious experimental work, and often non-optimal results. Thus, automatic planning methods which seek to optimize the setup degrees of freedom for a particular measurement are of special importance in this field. For automatic evaluation of an inspection, there exist typical evaluation metrics including but not limited to, the measurement uncertainty and the scan resolution. However, it is often not trivial how to combine different optimization criteria to optimize the setup based on the requirements. For example, it is not obvious how to compare an the result of an inspection with a high lateral resolution and a high uncertainty against another inspection, with a low lateral resolution but precise measurements. We propose to fuse the metrics through a probabilistic surface inference to quantify the amount of information gained by a specific setup configuration. To this end, we model the surface by a Gaussian random process and introduce a local surface inference method based on the local surface orientation. The measurement points delivered by a laser triangulation setup are simulated using real-time graphical simulations, and the uncertainty of single point measurements are estimated. This data is further used as input to the local inference method. The inference results are demonstrated for the inspection of the intake manifold of a cylinder head.

1 Introduction

In today's manufacturing processes, machine vision provides industries with innovative solutions towards the automation of the production quality assurance [MPZ+03]. Typical inspection techniques include laser triangulation, fringe projection, and deflectometry, as well as confocal microscopy and interferometry for high precision measurements [BLF15]. Different solutions are primarily chosen based on the inspection demands and the target surface properties. Based on the chosen technique, there are further degrees of freedom in the inspection setup, including among others, the position and orientation of the camera(s) and the illumination source(s), as well as the optical configuration of the participating devices [MBI+16b], which need to be set by the expert.

As the design space is high dimensional, a manual setup design necessitates a tedious trial and error process and a lot of engineering experience, which is often associated with high costs and can easily end up in a compromise between contrary requirements, or resort to a rule of thumb setup design. Moreover, to quantitatively evaluate the inspection, one needs to experimentally evaluate the inspection performance based on the specific target product and the available sensors, similar to the work by Feng et al. [FLX01c]. One of our intentions in this report is to derive a suitable comprehensive cost function based on the inspection requirements, to automatically design optimized machine vision prototypes for inspecting different products without the need to realize the setup. This prevents unnecessary costs and the tedious experimental work.

To automate the setup design process and to plan an optimized inspection, several sensor planning methods have been introduced in the literature [TTA+95], [Sco09], [GO16]. In these works, different evaluation metrics are considered and taken as optimization cost functions into account. The optimum surface coverage [TG95] is one of the main goals pursued in almost all planning methods. Other constraints such as depth of field, field of view, and resolution are also of interest [TTA+95]. More recent works also take the uncertainty of measurement into account [Sco09, GO16, MBI+16a].

For incorporating the metrics into an optimization framework, a few approaches have been proposed. One approach is to evaluate the metrics as constraints and try to fulfill them simultaneously [TTA+95]. Another approach is based on the computation of the *measurability matrix*, introduced by Tarbox [TG95]. This method is primarily based on a matrix data structure whose rows span the discretized surface points and columns span the discretized sensor view-points, and each matrix element indicates boolean fulfillment of the inspection constraints [Sco09] or a weighted sum of different inspection metrics [GO16]. A third approach is to consider different metrics as separate criteria optimized in a multi-objective optimization framework [DO05].

The evaluation criteria can be contradictory. This turns a multi-objective optimization more into choosing a trade-off between the goals. For example, increasing the distance leads to a broader sensor coverage but also increases the measurement uncertainty. Finding a suitable weighting between the goals is also not trivial and can easily lead to one metric dominating the other. For instance, it is difficult to compare an inspection with a high resolution but a high measurement uncertainty with another inspection with a lower resolution but also a lower uncertainty of measurement. For a dense sampling of the design space which is often high dimensional, the memory allocation demand for the measurability matrix is also prohibitive.

Our solution for a suitable metric fusion is to formulate the amount of *information* we obtain by each measurement, using a Bayesian inference framework. In this method, the measurement resolution and the corresponding uncertainties of the point measurements are fused together by the surface inference method. To this end, we model the target surface as a random process and adapt the problem to a Gaussian Process (GP) inference [RW06]. The measurement points delivered by each sensor view-point are simulated using real-time graphical simulations, augmented with an estimate of their corresponding measurement uncertainty, and further used in a GP learning framework to update the random process. The standard deviation of the updated random process (a posteriori process) actually indicates the amount of information that a specific sensor configuration delivers to us, and can be evaluated at each arbitrary point on the surface. The probabilistic surface inference method can be applied to all point-based inspection techniques such as the general group of structured-light scanning methods [BLF15].

2 Surface Inference

Most visual inspection techniques scan the target object through sampling the surface in a number of 3D points. Among different criteria discussed in the previous section, the quality of the scanned point cloud can be mainly characterized by the *scan resolution* and the respective *uncertainty* of each measured point [MBI+16b]. Figure 2.1 shows a 2D illustration of inspecting a surface with a number of point measurements, where each ellipse represents the uncertainty of each sampled point. Before we begin with formulating the surface inference, we briefly introduce these two properties.

Scan resolution indicates the local density of the points on the surface, or the lateral resolution of the measurement. Based on the object geometry and the relative distance of the surface points to the camera, the surface is in general inhomogeneously sampled. There can be parts unreachable by the illumination or occluded to the camera, which cause a local point density of zero. Therefore, the scan resolution property is an extended visibility metric, which not only encodes the measurablility of a surface part, but also its lateral resolution.

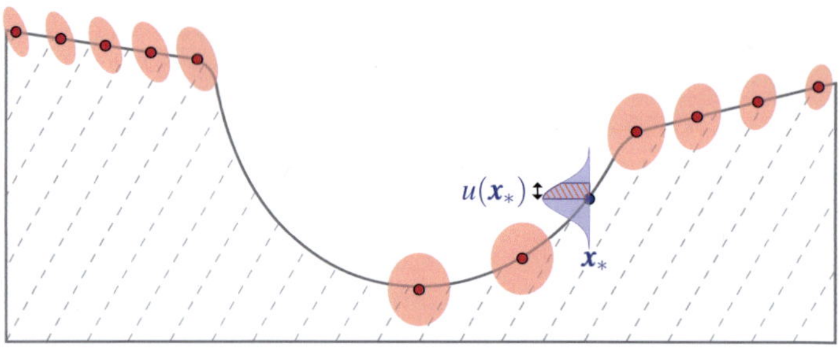

Figure 2.1: 2D illustration of surface inspection with noisy measurements. Red ellipses denote measurement uncertainties. $\boldsymbol{x}_*$ is an arbitrary point on the surface to be inferred, and $u(\boldsymbol{x}_*)$ indicates the inference uncertainty.

Measurement uncertainty is defined as the standard deviation of the measurement from the nominal value, which is an indication of the measurement reliability [gum08]. The ellipses in Figure 2.1 correspond to the uncertainty of each measurement point. In the case of 3D measurements, each point is subject to a 3D uncertainty. In our previous work [MBI$^+$16a], we have formulated a framework for probabilistic modeling and analytic propagation of the sources of uncertainty pertinent to a laser scanner. The sources of uncertainty include the uncertainty of the feature detection on the image, the setup geometrical positioning uncertainties, and the optical calibration uncertainties. We have approximated the resulting 3D uncertainty in each point measurement as a Gaussian distribution which corresponds to an ellipsoid (i.e. 3×3 covariance matrix).

The objective of surface inference is to merge these metrics and determine a probability distribution for the position of an arbitrary point $\boldsymbol{x}_*$ on the surface (see Figure 2.1), given the measurement data. In order to consider the contribution of the measured points to our degree of belief at the point $\boldsymbol{x}_*$, we apply a Bayesian framework. In such a framework, we always have a prior knowledge about the subject under study in the form of an a priori distribution [BS94]. In this case, the a priori distribution can be given based on the typical variations in the manufactured products. As new observations are made, our prior belief will be updated, and an a posteriori distribution is calculated based on the Bayes' law.

The a posteriori standard deviation $u(\boldsymbol{x}_*)$ indicates our remaining uncertainty at the point $\boldsymbol{x}_*$ after the surface has been measured. This way we can evaluate an inspection in terms of the amount of the new information it delivers to us about the surface compared to our prior knowledge. In this paper, we refer to $u(\boldsymbol{x}_*)$ as the *inference uncertainty*, which is in concrete words defined as the standard deviation of our prediction of the surface height $h(\boldsymbol{x}_*)$ at point $\boldsymbol{x}_*$.

Different constellations of the inspection setup deliver different sets of sampled points with different measurement uncertainties [MBI$^+$16a], which in turn result in different a posteriori distributions for the product surface. Based on the desired inspection requirements, one can evaluate the resulting a posteriori distributions along the surface and use it as an optimization criteria for the setup design.

Modeling each surface point as a random variable indicates that the whole surface is modeled by a stochastic process. A stochastic process is a collection of random variables $\{h(\boldsymbol{x})|\boldsymbol{x} \in D\}$ indexed by a set D [GWB97]. For a surface in 3D, D is a subset of the $\mathbb{R}^2$ space and $h(\boldsymbol{x})$ is a random variable corresponding to the height of the continuous 2D input $\boldsymbol{x}$.

In a 3D inspection, we measure the surface in a number of points $\{\tilde{\boldsymbol{x}}_i, \tilde{h}_i\}$ with $\tilde{\boldsymbol{x}}_i \in \mathbb{R}^2$ and $\tilde{h}_i = \tilde{h}(\tilde{\boldsymbol{x}}_i) \in \mathbb{R}$. Each point measurement is associated with a measurement uncertainty (covariance matrix) Σ_i, depicted as a red ellipse in Figure 2.1. We further define the pair $\{\tilde{X}, \tilde{\boldsymbol{h}}\}$ as a compact notation for referring to all measurement points. In machine learning terms, the measured data $\{\tilde{X}, \tilde{\boldsymbol{h}}\}$ is referred to as the training data. Inferring an arbitrary point $\boldsymbol{x}_*$ denotes computing the probability distribution $p(h_*|\tilde{X}, \tilde{\boldsymbol{h}})$ [RW06].

We distinguish between two different uncertainties in Figure 2.1. The red ellipses correspond to the measurement uncertainty due to the limited precision of the sensor. However, $u(\boldsymbol{x}_*)$ corresponds to the standard deviation of our prediction (our degree of belief) for the height of the point $\boldsymbol{x}_*$. The calculation of the a posteriori distribution of the surface using Gaussian Process is the main topic of the next section.

2.1 Surface Inference by Gaussian Process

A Gaussian Process (GP) [RW06] is a special variant of a stochastic process, and is widely used in many problems dealing with non-parametric function learning. In a Gaussian process, the joint distribution between each subset of $\{h(\boldsymbol{x}_1), ..., h(\boldsymbol{x}_k)\}$ is a multivariate Gaussian distribution [RW06]. This property gives the GP the nice feature to have a closed form solution for the desired conditional probability $p(h_*|\tilde{X}, \tilde{\boldsymbol{h}})$, using the standard Gaussian conditioning. This is one of the main reasons for the GP popularity in regression and classification problems.

A GP can be fully specified by its mean $\mu(\boldsymbol{x})$ and covariance function $c(\boldsymbol{x}, \boldsymbol{x}')$:

$$\mu(\boldsymbol{x}) = E[h(\boldsymbol{x})],$$

$$c(\boldsymbol{x}, \boldsymbol{x}') = E[(h(\boldsymbol{x}) - \mu(\boldsymbol{x}))(h(\boldsymbol{x}') - \mu(\boldsymbol{x}'))],$$

where E denotes the expectation operator. For a GP inference, the mean and the covariance function should be already given or assumed.

The covariance function and its free parameters are central in determining the GP. The type of the covariance function is usually chosen based on our understanding of the properties of the underlying function, such as its differentiability. The free parameters of the covariance function, (often referred to as the hyper-parameters [RW06]), control further properties such as the level of smoothness and the scale of the function. It is common to consider many processes as isotropic stationary processes and define the covariance function as a function of the Euclidean distance $c(r) = c(|\boldsymbol{x} - \boldsymbol{x'}|)$, or non-Euclidean distances. A comprehensive study of covariance functions is given by Rasmussen and Williams [RW06].

The desired a posteriori distribution $p(h_*|\tilde{X}, \tilde{\boldsymbol{h}})$ is another Gaussian distribution, derived by conditioning on the training data. The mean and the variance of the a posteriori distribution at the point $\boldsymbol{x}_*$ can be derived as given in Eq. (2.1) and (2.2) [RW06]. These equations are derived using the standard Gaussian conditioning.

$$\mu_* = \mu(\boldsymbol{x}_*) + \boldsymbol{k}_*[K + \sigma_h^2 I]^{-1}(\tilde{\boldsymbol{h}} - \boldsymbol{\mu}(\tilde{X})) \tag{2.1}$$

$$\sigma_*{}^2 = k_{**} - \boldsymbol{k}_*[K + \sigma_h^2 I]^{-1}\boldsymbol{k}_*^{\mathrm{T}} \tag{2.2}$$

In the above equations, $K \in \mathcal{R}^{N \times N}$ is a square matrix containing the pairwise covariance between N training data, $\boldsymbol{k}_* \in \mathcal{R}^{N \times 1}$ is a vector containing the covariance of the inference point $\boldsymbol{x}_*$ with the training data, I is the $N \times N$ identity matrix, and k_{**} is a single scalar given by $c(\boldsymbol{x}_*, \boldsymbol{x}_*)$, which is actually the variance of the prior distribution $p(h_*)$. The training points $\tilde{X}$ in these equations are considered noise-free, and their corresponding function values $\tilde{\boldsymbol{h}}$ are subject to an independent identically distributed (i.i.d.) noise with variance σ_h^2. The assumption of noise in Gaussian process is somehow different from that of our surface measurement, and for this reason we use the *Noisy Input Gaussian Process (NIGP)* method [And14] to integrate the 3D uncertainties in the GP.

In the application of surface inspection, the CAD product model can be directly used as the mean function $\mu(\boldsymbol{x})$. The a priori distribution for an inference point can be chosen based on the expert knowledge about the production variations (e.g. 10 mm standard deviation compared to the CAD model). Figure 2.2 shows the CAD model of a cylinder head.

The choice of the covariance function is however more complicated. It is important to note that the real surface to inspect is not the ideal CAD model of the product, but rather a complicated surface with different levels of detail. Figure 2.3 shows an illustration of a manufactured surface. This surface is ideally a plane; however, the manufactured surface can contain deviations from an ideal plane in several scales. The inspection resolution is actually the criteria to distinguish between the surface defects, which the inspection is supposed to identify, and the unavoidable surface roughness, which is not supposed to be detected as an error. It is therefore important to choose the covariance function which suits

Figure 2.2: The CAD model of a cylinder head.

reconstructing the surface upto the desired level of detail that we intend to inspect the surface with. This is usually achieved by suitably setting the parameters of the covariance function. The squared-exponential (SE) or the Gaussian function given in Eq. (2.3) is a very common choice for the covariance function in many applications. Many real rough surfaces are also shown to have a Gaussian auto-correlation function [BS87].

$$c(r) = \sigma_f^2 \, e^{\left(\frac{-r^2}{2l^2}\right)} \tag{2.3}$$

Most covariance functions are parameterized with at least two parameters. One parameter is a scale factor (in this case σ_f^2) indicating the maximum value of the function, or $c(0)$. This value should be set to the prior variance of the surface, or the variance of the a priori distribution, since we have $c(0) = c(\boldsymbol{x}_*, \boldsymbol{x}_*) = var(\boldsymbol{x}_*)$. Another parameter is the correlation length-scale (in this case the parameter l), which indicates the decaying behavior of the covariance function.

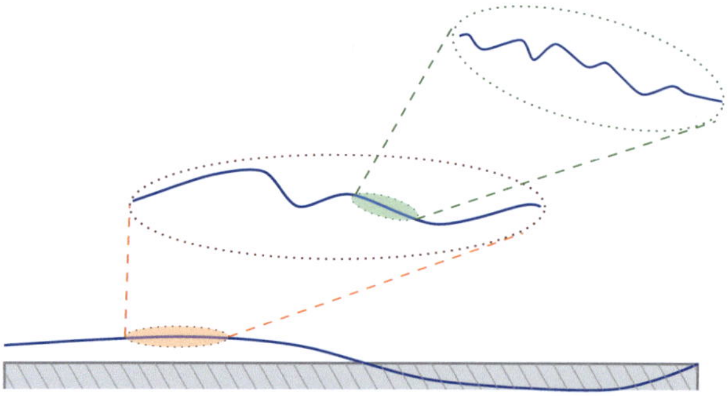

Figure 2.3: Surface defects at several levels of detail, in comparison to the ideal flat model.

This length-scale parameter mainly determines the level of detail reconstructed from the surface. Large length-scale values lead to a surface reconstructed with lower frequencies, whereas smaller values tend to reconstruct more details from the surface.

2.2 Local Inference

In this section we propose a local inference method for the inference of industrial product surfaces. As seen in equations (2.1) and (2.2), the calculation of the a posteriori mean and variance depends on the calculation of the inverse of an $N \times N$ matrix $K + \sigma_h^2 I$, with N being the number of the training points, i.e. measurement points, which is often a large value. Moreover, the inference variance σ_*^2 is always calculated along a particular axis, which is actually the axis along which the surface height h is defined. However, industrial products have surface complexities which make it almost impossible to define a function $h(\boldsymbol{x})$ which can define the whole surface; however, industrial surfaces can be locally well parameterized. As the last motivation for the local inference method, we are particularly interested to derive the surface inference uncertainty locally along the normal direction of the surface to better encode the deviations from the surface, and thus, we are interested in local transformations which rotates the surface along the local normal direction.

We justify the idea of a local inference by referring to the fact that all covariance functions decay monotonically with distance, except for some special cases like periodic functions which are not of interest for us. Therefore, for the inference of a point $\boldsymbol{x}_*$, only the measurement points inside a neighborhood radius r from the point can effectively contribute. The value of r can be directly derived from the covariance function, based on a low threshold, which directly depends on the correlation length-scale discussed previously. This brings us to the idea of a local inference, in which for each inference point of interest, we search for the measurement points inside the neighborhood and derive the inference based on the retrieved points, instead of considering all the points which actually do not contribute much. The local inference significantly improves the runtime performance, as only a limited set of effective points are considered for each inference.

In addition, we are also able to apply the desired local transformations on the retrieved points.

For applying the local transformation, we transform the set of points selected in a neighborhood to a new local coordinate frame by a rotation R, so that the transformed heights of the point h' align with the direction of the local surface normal vector. A 2D illustration of this transformation is depicted in Figure 2.4. The 3D ellipsoids Σ_i corresponding to the measurement uncertainty of each point will be also represented in the new coordinate frame by $R\Sigma_i R^{\mathrm{T}}$. Consequently, by applying the GP inference in the new coordinates, the inference uncertainty $u(\boldsymbol{x}_*)$ will be calculated along the h' direction which is parallel to the normal direction. This is desirable since the uncertainty will be always calculated along the local normal direction, indicating the deviations from the nominal model, independent of the complex changes of orientation along the whole surface. The neighborhood sphere in Figure 2.4 moves along the surface and at each point a local transformation and thus a local inference is applied. For the integration of the 3D measurement uncertainties in the GP, we use the *Noisy Input Gaussian Process (NIGP)* method [And14].

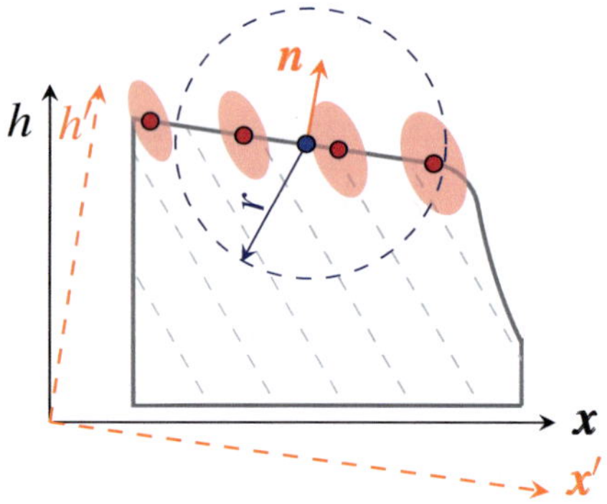

Figure 2.4: 2D illustration of the local inference. The local points are transformed towards the surface normal direction. h' will be parallel to the normal n and the $\boldsymbol{x}'$ axis will be parallel to the local linear approximation of the surface.

Figure 3.1: Intake manifold of a cylinder head segmented for surface inference.

3 Inference of a Cylinder Head Surface

In this section we apply the proposed probabilistic surface inference method to evaluate the inspection of a cylinder head using the laser triangulation method. The cylinder head is a geometrically complex product requiring a precise verification, and thus, it is considered as a challenging example for the planning problem. The cylinder head surface is in general not a differentiable surface; moreover, different parts of the model can be manufactured independently which indicates that the defects at some surface parts are not correlated to each other. Therefore, we have manually segmented the model into partially differentiable regions using the Blender software [Ble16], and apply the surface inference separately for each region. Figure 3.1 displays the segmented intake manifold of the cylinder head. Each color represents a separate segment whose inference is done separately.

Before we apply the inference, we simulate the image acquisition from each desired viewpoint and obtain the corresponding measured point cloud of the target. To simulate the image acquisition process, we use the Rasterization Simulation Library (RSL), which was also introduced in our previous report [BP15]. The graphical simulations are GPU-accelerated and can be performed very quickly even on commodity hardware. The simulation input includes the geometrical setup constellation, the laser properties such as wavelength, focal distance, divergence, and opening angle, the camera resolution, and above all the CAD model of the workpiece and frequency of image acquisition during the object movement. By the graphical simulations, we are able to obtain a 3D point cloud corresponding to each complete scan of the object, as well as single frame rendered images. Figure 3.2(a) displays the parameterization of the setup geometrical degrees of freedom in the RSL. Figure 3.2(b) is captured from the RSL environment and corresponds to the simulation of the cylinder head inspection for a particular constellation. More information regarding the physically-based simulation of a laser line and the RSL is given in our previous works [BMI+16] [MBI+16b].

We further augment the simulated points with their respective 3D measurement uncertainties, based on our previous work [MBI+16a]. In this work, the sources of uncertainty in a laser triangulation measurement are modeled and propagated to the output. We have considered a $0.2\ px$ standard deviation for the laser detection on the image and a $0.5\ mm$ standard deviation for the positioning of the whole setup (neglecting rotational and optical calibration uncertainties). This will be the input to the local inference method described in section 2.2.

We have applied the proposed inference method on the intake manifold of the cylinder head. Figure 3.3 shows the resulting uncertainty of the inference (standard deviation of the GP), for the inspection of the cylinder head corresponding to the constellation in Figure 3.2(b). We sample the model using the *Poisson disk sampling* method [CJW+09] to achieve sample points which evenly cover the surface, and the local inference method is then applied to each sampled point.

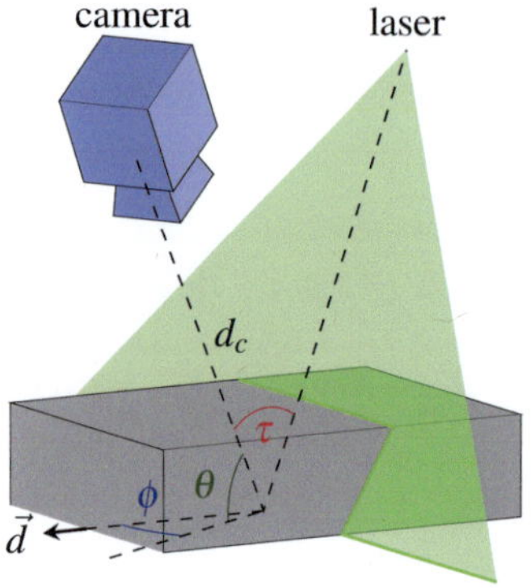

(a)

(b)

Figure 3.2: (a) Parameterization of the laser scanner setup geometry in RSL. The angle ϕ is defined w.r.t. the scan direction $\vec{d}$. (b) RSL interactive environment for the simulation of the constellation with parameters $\{\ \theta = 84°, \phi = 80°, \tau = 5°, dc = 0.4m\}$.

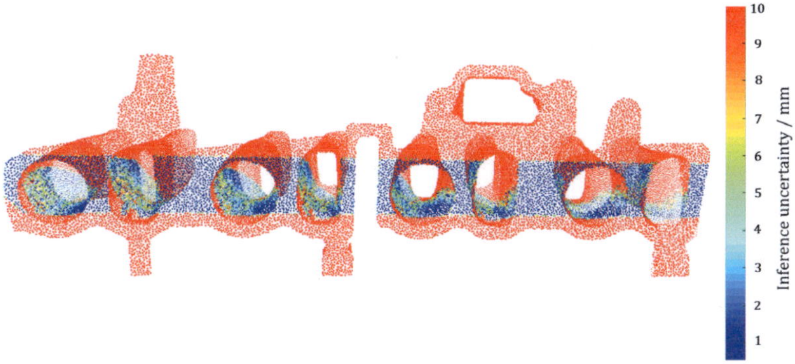

Figure 3.3: Inference uncertainty for the inspection of the cylinder head intake manifold.

For the GP inference, the SE covariance function is used and an a priori standard deviation (σ_f) of $10\ mm$, and a correlation length-scale of $l = 0.6\ mm$ is considered for the surface. The scan simulation contains 700 frames in which the cylinder is moved by $1\ mm$ per frame. The simulated camera captures 512×512 px images with a vertical field of view of $45°$.

In Figure 3.3, the red regions with an inference uncertainty of $10\ mm$ correspond to regions which have not been measured by the inspection, due to being out of the field of view or not reached by the laser. Therefore, the prior standard deviation is not updated at those parts. Based on the lateral resolution and the uncertainty of the measurement at other regions, the surface uncertainty has been reduced.

The inference uncertainty along the surface can be considered as a suitable cost function for the optimization of the setup design, as this metric already takes the lateral resolution and the measurement uncertainty into account and indicates the degree of the *informativeness* of the inspection, in comparison to our prior knowledge about the surface. For the optimization, one can consider the sum of the uncertainties along the surface, or the maximum uncertainty, or other suitable statistics, and optimize the surface inspection parameters (both geometrical and optical) in an optimization framework.

4 Conclusion and Future Work

The probabilistic inference method discussed in this report fuses the measurement uncertainty and the resolution into a metric that indicates the adequacy of the inspection, by formulating the information a measurement delivers to us compared to our prior information about the surface. This means that the surface inference method actually derives the amount of *new* information that the measurement has delivered. This metric can be particularly useful to be used in an optimization framework to determine the setup degrees of freedom, by minimizing the a posteriori variance along the surface.

Our approach for the future work will be primarily to incorporate the proposed inference method in an optimization framework. In addition, we also attempt to extend our model of the measurement uncertainty. The estimated measurement uncertainties are based on modeling the sources of stochastic noise in the measurement; while other sources of error such as multiple reflections of the laser on the surface are not considered. In the future, we will also attempt to approximate these sources of error in the simulations and take them into account for the optimization.

Bibliography

[And14] Andrew Mchutchon. *Nonlinear Modelling and Control using Gaussian Processes*. Dissertation, Department of Engineering, University of Cambridge, 2014.

[Ble16] Blender Online Community. *Blender - a 3D modelling and rendering package*. Blender Foundation, 2016.

[BLF15] Jürgen Beyerer, Fernando Puente León, and Christian Frese. *Machine Vision: Automated Visual Inspection: Theory, Practice and Applications*. Springer, 2015.

[BMI+16] Stephan Bergmann, Mahsa Mahammadikaji, Stephan Irgenfried, Heinz Wörn, Jürgen Beyerer, and Carsten Dachsbacher. A Phenomenological Approach to Integrating Gaussian Beam Properties and Speckle into a Physically-Based Renderer. In Matthias Hullin, Marc Stamminger, and Tino Weinkauf, editors, *Vision, Modeling & Visualization*. The Eurographics Association, 2016.

[BP15] Jürgen Beyerer and Alexey Pak, editors. *Proceedings of the 2015 Joint Workshop of Fraunhofer IOSB and Institute for Anthropomatics, Vision and Fusion Laboratory*, Karlsruher Schriften zur Anthropomatik, Triberg-Nussbach, Deutschland, July 2015. KIT Scientific Publishing.

[BS87] Petr Beckmann and Andre Spizzichino. The scattering of electromagnetic waves from rough surfaces. *Norwood, MA, Artech House, Inc., 1987, 511 p.*, 1987.

[BS94] Jos M. Bernardo and Adrian F. M. Smith. *Bayesian Theory*. John Wiley & Sons, Inc, Hoboken, NJ, USA, 1994.

[CJW+09] D. Cline, S. Jeschke, K. White, A. Razdan, and P. Wonka. Dart throwing on surfaces. *Computer Graphics Forum*, 28(4):1217–1226, 2009.

[DO05] E. Dunn and G. Olague. Pareto optimal camera placement for automated visual inspection. In *IEEE/RSJ International Conference on Intelligent Robots and Systems*, pages 3821–3826, 2005.

[FLX01c] Hsi-Yung Feng, Yixin Liu, and Fengfeng Xi. Analysis of digitizing errors of a laser scanning system. *Precision Engineering*, 25(3):185–191, 2001.

[GO16] Marc Gronle and Wolfgang Osten. View and sensor planning for multi-sensor surface inspection. *Surface Topography: Metrology and Properties*, 4(2), 2016.

[gum08] Evaluation of Measurement data–Guide to the Expression of Uncertainty in Measurement. JCGM 100:2008, 2008.

[GWB97] Paul W. Goldberg, Christopher K. I. Williams, and Christopher M. Bishop. Regression with input-dependent noise: A gaussian process treatment. *Advances in neural information processing systems*, 10:493–499, 1997.

[MBI+16a] Mahsa Mohammadikaji, Stephan Bergmann, Stephan Irgenfried, Jürgen Beyerer, Carsten Dachsbacher, and Heinz Wörn. A framework for uncertainty propagation in 3d shape measurement using laser triangulation. In *2016 IEEE International Instrumentation and Measurement Technology Conference Proceedings*, pages 1–6. IEEE, 2016.

[MBI+16b] Mahsa Mohammadikaji, Stephan Bergmann, Stephan Irgenfried, Jürgen Beyerer, Carsten Dachsbacher, and Heinz Wörn. Performance characterization in automated optical inspection using cad models and graphical simulations. In *XXX Messtechnisches Symposium*. DE GRUYTER, 2016.

[MPZ+03] Elias N Malamas, Euripides GM Petrakis, Michalis Zervakis, Laurent Petit, and Jean-Didier Legat. A survey on industrial vision systems, applications and tools. *Image and vision computing*, 21(2):171–188, 2003.

[RW06] Carl Edward Rasmussen and Christopher K. I. Williams. *Gaussian processes for machine learning*. Adaptive computation and machine learning. MIT Press, 2006.

[Sco09] William R. Scott. Model-based view planning. *Machine Vision and Applications*, 20(1):47–69, 2009.

[TG95] G. H. Tarbox and S. N. Gottschlich. Planning for complete sensor coverage in inspection. *Computer Vision and Image Understanding*, 61(1):84–111, 1995.

[TTA+95] Konstantinos Tarabanis, Roger Y Tsai, Peter K Allen, et al. The mvp sensor planning system for robotic vision tasks. *Robotics and Automation, IEEE Transactions on*, 11(1):72–85, 1995.

Anomaly Detection in Industrial Networks: *An Introduction*

Ankush Meshram

Vision and Fusion Laboratory
Institute for Anthropomatics
Karlsruhe Institute of Technology (KIT), Germany
ankush.meshram@kit.edu

Technical Report IES-2016-05

Abstract: With the advent of 21st Century, we stepped into the fourth industrial revolution of cyber physical systems. The industrial components are modular and capable of taking decentralized decisions in real time. The processes can be virtualized and automated through inter-operable service oriented components connected in a network. Therefore, there is need of secured network systems and intrusion detection systems in order to detect network attacks. Use of machine learning for anomaly detection in industrial networks faces challenges which restricts its large-scale commercial deployment. A roadmap is proposed to overcome the challenges. Real world network traffic for an industrial production is generated by IT Security Laboratory at Fraunhofer IOSB. The various attack vectors can be implemented under these circumstances and an adaptive hybrid analysis would reduce the errors of an intrusion detection system. Alarm correlation could be performed for semantic descriptions of detected results to network operator.

1 Introduction

The 21st Century is witnessing the *fourth* industrial revolution since the *first* revolution in the 18th century of manufacturing mechanization powered by water and steam. Invention of electricity led to the *second* revolution of mass production with introduction of assembly lines in the final third of the 19th Century. The *third* industrial revolution was driven by developments in the field of electronics and information technology in mid 20th Century where the complex tasks within manufacturing industry are automated leading to increased production rates. Recent innovative technological developments of information and communication technology (ICT), sensor technology, network communications, virtualization of manufacturing processes and data analysis with Big Data analytics and cloud computing enables mass customization in industrial production. Efficiency is highly increased with real time vertical integration of manufacturing systems with business processes within factories and horizontal integration of value chains.

The goal of combining production methods with state-of-the-art ICT to create value chains to serve specific needs of consumers faces certain challenges. These challenges range from standardization of communication within factories to legally securing the sensitive information pertaining to various actors involved. To overcome the challenges and guide the digitization of industry to its success, national/international initiatives such as *Platform Industrie 4.0*, *Alliance Industrie du Futur*, *Industrial Internet Consortium* by Germany, France, USA, respectively, have been started.

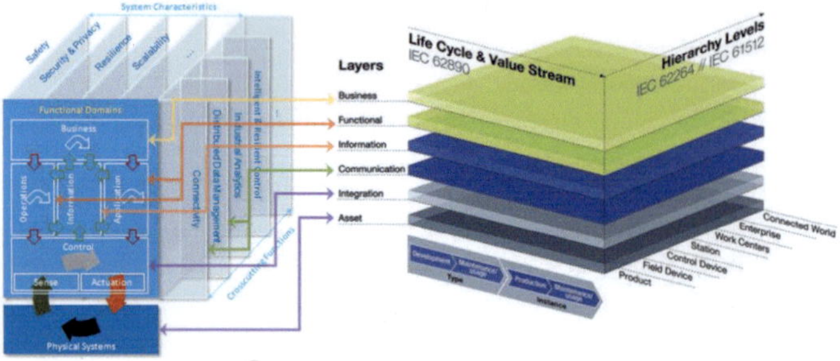

Figure 1.1: RAMI 4.0 vertical layers be mapped to IIRA viewpoints

Industry and academic institutions are working together to strengthen the research and development of technologies of the *fourth* industrial revolution. The Reference Architectural Model for Industrie 4.0 (RAMI 4.0) is the implementation strategy from *Platform Industrie 4.0* drawn upon existing standards such as

IEC 62890, IEC 62264, IEC 61512. It is a three-dimensional model (Fig. 1.1) grouping vertical networking between production components, end-to-end engineering across the value stream and horizontal dynamic creation of value added networks beyond individual factory locations. The vertical axis, *Layers*, consists of layers to represent various perspectives similar to IT thinking of splitting up complex projects into manageable clusters. The left-hand horizontal axis, *Life Cycle & Value Stream*, represents life cycle of systems or products with the value streams it contains, as "Type" and "Instance". The right-hand horizontal axis, *Hierarchy Levels*, represents the functional hierarchy within factories/plants, which is different from hierarchical levels of classical automation pyramid. The Industrial Internet Reference Architecture (IIRA) model developed by *Industrial Internet Consortium* is based on ISO/IEC/IEEE 42010:2011 standard. It aims to describe system properties from viewpoints of system users, operators, owners, developers, and the technicians maintaining and servicing the systems. These viewpoints correspond to business, usage, functional and implementation. Each viewpoint can be compared to respective layers on the vertical axis of RAMI 4.0 [4.016a].

The key aspect in the implementation of Industrie 4.0 is seamless transfer and real-time availability of information across the entire value stream through the application-oriented networking of all instances. According to [4.016b], network-based communication is the integral part for transformation of the classical industrial production pyramid into an integrated network of distributed systems. It comprises all the technologies,networks and protocols needed for communication among multiple Industrie 4.0 components. It would allow applications to negotiate end-to-end communication via Industrie 4.0-compliant interfaces for self-configuration of production systems.

Security, availability and quality of service (QoS) are the basic requirements of network-based communication. Securing network and data, identities of users/operators and ensuring functional security of systems comprises security requirement. The availability of processes and data in real-time and its desired utilization is the most crucial requirement in Industrie 4.0. Quality of service encompasses latency requirement with reliability of data transfer at the required data rate.

A variety of wired and wireless network communication standards have been developed or are in development. GSM, 3G or LTE networks are instances of mobile networks used to interconnect widely distributed or mobile assets. For networking of stationary endpoints, such as several distributed business locations, the state-of-the-art technology is secured connection through virtual private networks (VPN) with fibre-optic cabling. Industrial communication systems are based on decades old fieldbus protocols such as PROFIBUS and recently developed Ethernet-based protocols such as PROFINET. These wired protocols are used in production cells of manufacturing industries with high reliability and latency requirements. Wireless protocols such as WirelessHART also exist, however,they fail to meet latency and reliability requirements. Distributed Data Service (DDS) and OPC Unified Architecture (OPC UA) are industrial Machine-to-Machine (M2M) communication protocols enabling interoperability between devices, machines and systems. DDS aims for fast data exchange with deterministic communication within the systems. OPC UA focuses on interoperability while offering security and configurable access control to interfaces and data.

Modern production lines are highly networked. Their controllers and embedded systems communicate with each other independently, cloud-based planning systems calculate tasks and machine utilization, plant operators monitor and control the system remotely, maintenance staff can access and change the plant's configuration from anywhere on the planet. Today's protection measures for production plants must reach far beyond the factory site. Attackers can infiltrate and manipulate systems; malware can put subsystems out of action, potentially causing significant material damage, not to mention health risks and injuries. Cyber attacks on production plants were an issue long before Stuxnet, Duqu and Havex. With projects such as Industrie 4.0, the connectivity of production networks within companies and even with external partners will increase over the coming years. To protect against damage and production stoppages, suitable measures to prevent security incidents are urgently needed. One aspect of security is the monitoring of network traffic to detect anomalies that might be caused by cyber attacks on the production lines. In this paper we present a roadmap for the use of machine learning for anomaly detection in industrial networks. We propose solutions for the need of real world network traffic, an adaptive hybrid analysis to reduce error rates in diverse network traffic and alarm correlation for semantic description of detection results to the network operator.

The report is structured as follows. Section 2 motivates the need of cybersecurity in industrial networks to tackle threats to critical infrastructures and discusses available solutions in the form of Intrusion Detection Systems. Section 3 outlines the challenges of using machine learning techniques to detect anomalies in industrial networks and its large-scale commercial deployment. In section 4, we present the roadmap to find plausible solutions to all the challenges with an application suite and conclude the report.

2 Cybersecurity in Industrial Networks

Lack of trust in network-based communication between companies leads to security concerns, hence a major hindrance in the successful exchange and processing of information. Critical infrastructures at national level need to be secured against threats to industrial networks. The security objectives for secured network-based communications can be summarized, in order of priority, as availability, integrity, confidentiality, authentication, authorization, auditability, nonrepudiability and protection from third parties [DNVHC05]. Exploitation of network vulnerabilities resulting from violations of one or more security objectives can be termed as an attack. Attacks can be classified as internal threats originating within the company and external attacks where adversary is exploiting from outside the company network. Common types of attacks are Distributed Denial-of-Service(DDoS), eavesdropping, Man-in-the-Middle, virus/trojan/worm and breaking into a system. DDoS aims to violate availability of the system and eavesdropping violates confidentiality of the communication. In the Man-in-the-Middle attack, the attacker eavesdrops the communication channel and modify exchanged messages violating confidentiality and integrity objectives. Virus/trojan/worm bypasses authentication and authorization to inject and execute attacker's malicious code. Violations of authentication and authorization results in the attacker breaking into a system overcoming confidentiality and integrity objectives. The adversaries have become more skilled and knowledgeable, repeatedly attacking the systems and posing as a Advanced Persistent Threat (APT). Stuxnet, Shamoon/W32.DistTrack, Flame/Flamer/Skywiper are some examples of sophisticated APTs [KL14] making the network security crucial than ever before.

Security vulnerabilities in industrial networks have been detected, analyzed and their solutions have been formulated into a network security design principle of 'defense in depth' [SFS11]. Security is implemented at all the layers of communication network, with each layer isolating subsequent layers from external threats. The outermost layer of 'defense in depth' prevents unauthorized access to network from external sources. To restrict industrial network access only to engineers, control operators and business network, Firewalls are used, and remote access is secured using Virtual Private Networks (VPNs). To further tighten the security between business and industrial networks, a DeMilitarised Zone (DMZ) firewall configuration is utilized where two firewalls are placed in series between the networks. Equipment shared between business and industrial networks is placed within DMZ for access avoiding direct communication attempts between the networks. Unauthorized operation of network equipment through physical access could also damage the network functionality. Preventive measures such as password-protection on every device, blocking of unused ports on switches and routers, periodic updates of installed software and operating system on devices need to be taken. These authorization measures are collectively referred as 'hardening the equipment'. Communication channels of the network need to be secured to maintain data confidentiality, integrity and authentication. However, application of cryptographic algorithms to communication channels, as done in commercial networks, is currently a topic of research. As security threats evolve with technological developments in security algorithms, the older industrial equipment lacks the capacity to be up-to-date within real-time requirements. Formulation of an effective security policy requires analysis of network security policies, network equipment, existing networks and network protocols to detect and mitigate vulnerabilities. Intrusion Detection System aims to address all these requirements through detection of known attack patterns and/or unusual behavior of system or network.

Intrusion Detection System (IDS) technologies can be classified based on types of events being monitored and point of deployment as Host-based (HIDS), Network-based (NIDS) and based on Network Behavior Analysis (NBA) [SM07]. HIDS monitors characteristics of a single host and events occurring within the host. NIDS analyzes (wireless) network segments/devices for network and application protocol activity, while NBA examines network traffic to identify unusual traffic flows and policy violations. IDS technologies use different methodologies for detecting intrusions/incidents, which are primarily classified as signature-based, anomaly-based, and stateful protocol analysis. Signature-based detection compares known threat signatures against observed events to identify incidents. However, it is ineffective at detecting unknown and multi-event attacks. Anomaly-based detection compares normal activity profile against observed events to identify significant deviations. It is very effective at detecting previously unknown attacks, however unable to capture the complex and dynamic real world activity profile leading to high false positives rates. Stateful protocol analysis compares current protocol activity against predefined protocol profile activity to identify deviations. It lacks robustness as every protocol specification is vendor specific and analysis becomes obsolete with minute changes to the specification.

Anomaly-based intrusion detection systems for industrial networks have been widely studied with regards to unpredictable nature of network traffic. The approach consists of two phases: a training phase to define normal network traffic profile, and a testing phase where the learned profile is used to classify new data. There are huge number of techniques proposed for anomaly detection which can be grouped as statistical, knowledge-based and machine learning based [SM07, BG15, CBK09, PP07]. Univariate models, multivariate models and time-series analysis are generally used for statistical detection of anomalies. For knowledge-based anomaly detection, finite state machines, description languages and expert systems have been proposed and evaluated. Machine learning based techniques also encompasses data mining techniques which are summarized as fuzzy logic, bayesian networks, clustering, markov models, genetic algorithms, neural networks and support vector machines.

3 Anomaly Detection in Industrial Networks

Network monitoring is employed at strategic points within the network for intrusion detection. Wired and wireless communications between network devices are analyzed by intrusion detection system to find anomalies in the network traffic. Anomaly Detection in Industrial Networks (ADIN) analyzes packet data of network traffic and network flow characteristics for detection of abnormalities [BG15]. Each network data packet is a standard Ethernet frame of maximum 1518 bytes length with 8 bytes reserved for preamble, 12 bytes for destination and source MAC addresses, 2 bytes for frame type description, 46 - 1500 bytes for payload and last 4 bytes for cyclic redundancy check. The features of data varies with the communication protocol being used. Network flow characteristics are statistical features derived from raw network traffic packets based on certain parameters such as number of packets, window size, etc.

Anomaly detection in industrial networks using machine learning has been an active area of research for long time with some promising outcomes. However, it hasn't witnessed the large-scale commercial deployment compared to other domains of machine learning applications such as recommendation systems, natural language translation, spam detection. It stems from the fact that the domain of network intrusion detection system is complex and sensitive to high rate of false positives. [SP10] points out the challenges of applying machine learning to detect anomalies on network traffic, reiterated here as outlier detection, high cost of errors, semantic gap, and diversity of network traffic.

A. Outlier Detection: Since Dorothy Denning's proposal of anomaly detection for intrusion detection systems in 1986 [Den87], different machine learning models have been proposed and evaluated on published data sets such as DARPA 1999 [LHF$^+$00], KDD 1999 [Cup99]. However, [TBLG09] reported shortcomings of these data sets leading to inaccuracies of learned models. The quality of 'outlier' or abnormal activity detection in network traffic highly depends on the class separation of training data set for the learning model. Access to real world traffic data with "normal" activity and different attacks is restricted because of proprietary issues within industry. Data security and its protection is a major concern for any industry, which leads to ineffectiveness of learning models when deployed in real world.

B. High Cost of Errors: Errors in intrusion detection have expensive operational costs for any production system. A false positive would utilize an analyst's expensive time for in-depth inspection of reported system's activity only to find it benign. It could also lead to partial/complete shutdown of the production system bearing huge financial losses. A false negative would underplay a security breach making system vulnerable to serious damage, externally or intrinsically. As stated in [SP10], *even a single compromised system can seriously undermine the integrity of the IT infrastructure.*

C. Diversity of Network Traffic: Network traffic varies highly when observed over short interval period. The frequent variability in the network activity amounts to instability in establishing "normal" activity profile for a baseline.

The extracted features for detection turns out be ineffective under these circumstances. The traffic diversity is exhibited by both packet-level and application-level features. Aggregation over longer time period has been suggested to reduce the diversity of traffic.

D. Semantic Gap: Interpretation of reported results by intrusion detection systems to the network operators is usually inconclusive. Usually the deviation from normal profile activity is reported without explaining what it means (semantics) for system's status. It doesn't differentiate between "abnormal activity" and "attacks" contributing to longer duration of system diagnosis especially in case of a false positive. The basic challenge in reducing the semantic gap between network operator and the reported result is finding the correlation between learning model features and semantics of the network.

4 Roadmap

In order to overcome the challenges mentioned in previous section, we propose "*Anomaly Detection in Industrial Networks Suite (ADIN Suite)*" consisting of components for real world network traffic generation, adaptive hybrid analysis, and alarm correlation with knowledge-based explanation to network operators. Each component and challenges it addresses is briefly explained in following subsections.

4.1 Network Traffic Generation

IT Security Laboratory for industrial control systems at Fraunhofer IOSB, Karlsruhe [PKMH16] allows development and testing of industrial components for security research and training of IT security professionals. It has real network hardware components and highly flexible virtual environment for setting up real world production facilities. It also offers flexibility for testing the future networking technologies and protocols. As demonstrated by the attack case study in the paper, real world network attack on production processes can be performed in real time and detection facility is provided within the virtual infrastructure. Passive monitoring is performed within the laboratory setup to avoid unexpected behavior of the system, and collect normal activity of network traffic. Hence, it addresses the challenge of data collection with class separations, Sec.3.A. The classification of attack vectors for network intrusion and their implementation is underway. The data generated from IT Security Laboratory will be used for anomaly detection of multiple attacks in real time by hybrid analysis component of *ADIN Suite*.

4.2 Adaptive Hybrid Analysis

An adaptive hybrid network intrusion detection system would resolve the instability of learning models in response to variable network traffic behavior, Sec.3.B and Sec.3.C. The need to retrain the learning model every time the semantics of network environment changes would be diminished. Every attack type mentioned in Sec. 2 can be observed in the various network traffic characteristics such as throughput, average duration of flow between endpoints, networking protocol, etc. [Aho11]. Each network traffic characteristic can be uniquely analyzed on the extracted features. The temporal feature of network can be analyzed to determine the latency in the deterministic communication between production components. *Network characteristic analysis* captures the sequential aspect of the data and replay attacks explicitly. The payload of packet data in industrial communication varies with respect to industrial communication protocol being used. However, payload needs to be dissected to locate the process data it contains. *Process data analysis or packet inspection* detects the Man-in-the-Middle attack explicitly. Eavesdropping and breaking into a system can be detected by the *violations of security policies* while connecting to the network.

4.3 Alarm Correlation

The result of hybrid analysis components can be correlated to determine the severity of incidents being reported. These alarm correlations can be learned over time or set by an expert into semantically appropriate knowledge representation. The network operator can perform better diagnosis with additional information to reported deviations, hence reducing the system downtime in the case of false positives.

5 Conclusion

The paper outlines the roadmap, Figure 4.1, in finding the solutions to challenges of large scale implementation of anomaly detection in industrial networks using machine learning as an application suite named 'ADIN Suite'. The suite offers generation of real world network traffic through IT Security Laboratory at Fraunhofer IOSB, Karlsruhe where attack vectors can be implemented on production processes. An adaptive hybrid analysis approach inspects various network traffic characteristics for detection of different types of attacks. The alarm correlation module determines the severity of anomalies with knowledge-based explanation to network operator for efficient diagnosis.

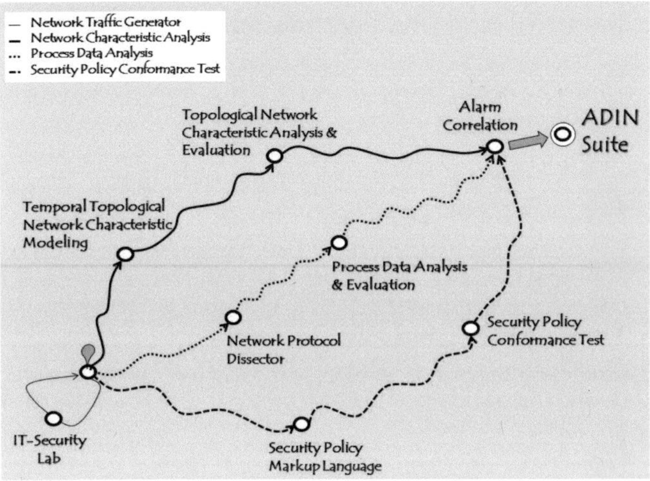

Figure 4.1: Roadmap to ADIN Suite

Bibliography

[4.016a] Platform Industrie 4.0. Cooperation between plattform industrie 4.0 and industrial internet consortium. 2016.

[4.016b] Platform Industrie 4.0. Network-based communication for industrie 4.0. Discussion paper, Federal Ministry for Economic Affairs and Energy (BMWi), Germany, 2016.

[Aho11] Pasi Ahonen. Constructing network security monitoring systems. *Vtt Research Notes*, 2011.

[BG15] Anna L Buczak and Erhan Guven. A survey of data mining and machine learning methods for cyber security intrusion detection. *IEEE Communications Surveys & Tutorials*, 18(2):1153–1176, 2015.

[CBK09] Varun Chandola, Arindam Banerjee, and Vipin Kumar. Anomaly detection: A survey. *ACM computing surveys (CSUR)*, 41(3):15, 2009.

[Cup99] KDD Cup. Dataset. *available at the following website http://kdd. ics. uci. edu/databases/kddcup99/kddcup99. html*, 1999.

[Den87] Dorothy E. Denning. An intrusion-detection model. *IEEE TRANSACTIONS ON SOFTWARE ENGINEERING*, 13(2):222–232, 1987.

[DNVHC05] Dacfey Dzung, Martin Naedele, Thomas P Von Hoff, and Mario Crevatin. Security for industrial communication systems. *Proceedings of the IEEE*, 93(6):1152–1177, 2005.

[KL14] Eric D Knapp and Joel Thomas Langill. *Industrial Network Security: Securing critical infrastructure networks for smart grid, SCADA, and other Industrial Control Systems*. Syngress, 2014.

[LHF+00] Richard Lippmann, Joshua W Haines, David J Fried, Jonathan Korba, and Kumar Das. The 1999 darpa off-line intrusion detection evaluation. *Computer networks*, 34(4):579–595, 2000.

[PKMH16] S. Pfrang, J. Kippe, D. Meier, and C. Haas. Design and Architecture of an Industrial IT Security Lab. In *TRIDENTCOM 2016 - Proceedings of the 11th International Conference on Testbeds and research infrastructures for the development of networks & communities (to appear)*, 2016.

[PP07] Animesh Patcha and Jung-Min Park. An overview of anomaly detection techniques: Existing solutions and latest technological trends. *Computer networks*, 51(12):3448–3470, 2007.

[SFS11] Keith Stouffer, Joe Falco, and Karen Scarfone. Guide to industrial control systems (ics) security. *NIST special publication*, 800(82):16–16, 2011.

[SM07] Karen Scarfone and Peter Mell. Guide to intrusion detection and prevention systems (idps). *NIST special publication*, 800(2007):94, 2007.

[SP10] Robin Sommer and Vern Paxson. Outside the closed world: On using machine learning for network intrusion detection. In *2010 IEEE symposium on security and privacy*, pages 305–316. IEEE, 2010.

[TBLG09] Mahbod Tavallaee, Ebrahim Bagheri, Wei Lu, and Ali-A Ghorbani. A detailed analysis of the kdd cup 99 data set. In *Proceedings of the Second IEEE Symposium on Computational Intelligence for Security and Defence Applications 2009*, 2009.

Next on Stage: 'MC ViSi' – a Machine Vision Simulation Framework

Johannes Meyer

Vision and Fusion Laboratory
Institute for Anthropomatics
Karlsruhe Institute of Technology (KIT), Germany
johannes.meyer@kit.edu

Technical Report IES-2016-06

Abstract: Machine vision systems are used in diverse kinds of industries. They are employed in automobiles for the detection and protection of pedestrians, in visual inspection systems to ensure the quality of produced goods etc. The parameters of such systems result in many degrees of freedom. Determining the optimal setting of these parameters usually represents a time-consuming task that has to be performed empirically. This article introduces a software framework consisting of multiple plugins for the physically based rendering suite Mitsuba. By means of combining the single framework components, the sensor signals of arbitrary machine vision systems can be simulated for synthetic scenes consisting of objects having complex 3D geometries and the design process of the whole system can be streamlined.

1 Introduction

In many industrial fields, thousands or even millions of high quality products are produced every day. In order to ensure the produced goods' quality, they are usually visually inspected. Often, the visual inspection is performed by human workers. However, since this is a fatiguing task for humans, they may oversee defects what could have disastrous consequences. Therefore there exists a huge demand for automated visual inspection systems.

A visual inspection system usually contains one or more sensors and illumination sources. In order to build an effective inspection system, the components have to be well adapted to the inspection problem on hand. For example, the focal length and the magnification of a camera lens, the size of the sensor, the angle, color and intensity of the illumination sources and the relative placement and orientation of all components with respect to each other have to match in order to allow a successful processing of the acquired sensor images. Often, an expert determines the optimal parameters via time consuming experiments.

The procedure of adjusting the degrees of freedom of a visual inspection system can be streamlined using computer simulations. By employing accurate models of the employed sensors and light sources, a suitable physically based rendering framework and CAD models of the objects under test, the experiments can be simulated. Furthermore, quality metrics concerning the resulting sensor images, e.g., contrast, can be used to automatically evaluate batches of different parameter sets. In total, such a simulation framework is a potential basis of a method allowing to efficiently and accurately determine the optimal parameters of visual inspection systems.

This article presents *MC ViSi*, a novel bundle of plugins for the physically based rendering framework Mitsuba [Wen10]. Indeed, the Mitsuba framework already includes plugins like an entocentric camera, a telecentric camera, a collimated beam source etc.. However, the parameterization of these plugins is focused on computer graphics applications, e.g., by using terms like the field of view, focus distance and clipping planes. In contrast, for components employed in machine vision applications, parameters like the focal length, the image distance, the sensor element size, etc. are common. MC ViSi extends the Mitsuba framework by appropriately parameterized plugins modeling components of sensor and illumination classes that are often employed in machine vision systems for visual inspection. Particularly, the bundle includes concepts of sensors and light sources involved in light field imaging and processing. Recent research investigates the suitability of such components in novel approaches for the visual inspection of transparent objects [MLB16b, MLB16a, MGLB16]. For such applications, the direction of captured light rays can exhibit important information, e.g., about scattering defects present in a test object. Section 3 introduces the core components of the Mitsuba renderer and briefly explains how a sensor image is rendered.

2 Related work

The idea of using simulation frameworks to support the design of automated visual inspection systems has been adopted by different groups of researchers.

In [NZL16], Nürnberg et al. employed a rendering framework in order to optimize the parameters of a computational camera used for depth estimations.

The group of Mohammadikaji et al. [BM+16, MBI+16] proposed an uncertainty propagation framework for finding optimal arrangements in a laser triangulation setup by means of precisely simulating the laser's speckle effects and the reflectance properties of the investigated test object.

Irgenfried et al. [ITW11, IDW14] developed a software framework capable of optimizing the parameters of image processing routines involved in a visual inspection process. Therefore they simulated the inspection scene using both realtime and photorealistic renderers.

The suitability of different combinations of novel optical setups and subsequent image processing algorithms for finding defects in transparent materials has been shown by Meyer et al. by also employing a simulation framework [MGLB16, MLB16a, MLB16c, MLB16b].

3 Basic rendering framework

The plugins of the MC ViSi package are based on the Mitsuba rendering framework. Figure 3.1 shows the core components of Mitsuba and how they interact with each other. In order to render an image, the main component, i.e., the renderer, passes a sensor sample and, if required, also an aperture sample to the sensor component. For example, the aperture sample is needed by plugins modeling conventional cameras, where every pixel integrates incident light rays coming from multiple directions. The sensor component determines the ray of sight corresponding to the two samples. The renderer traces the ray of sight through the scene. All objects and light sources that should be rendered are contained in the scene. The ray of sight might get reflected, scattered or absorbed while being traced. Whenever the ray hits a light source, the renderer passes the 3D position of the intersection together with the direction of incidence to the respective component. The involved light source plugin determines and returns the spectrum and intensity of the light that it emits into the queried direction. The renderer calculates the final radiance corresponding to the current sensor sample by propagating the spectrum back along the traversed optical path and by taking the reflectance characteristics of all involved surfaces into account. The film component successively aggregates all pairs of sensor samples and radiances and transforms them into the final sensor image as soon as the rendering process has finished.

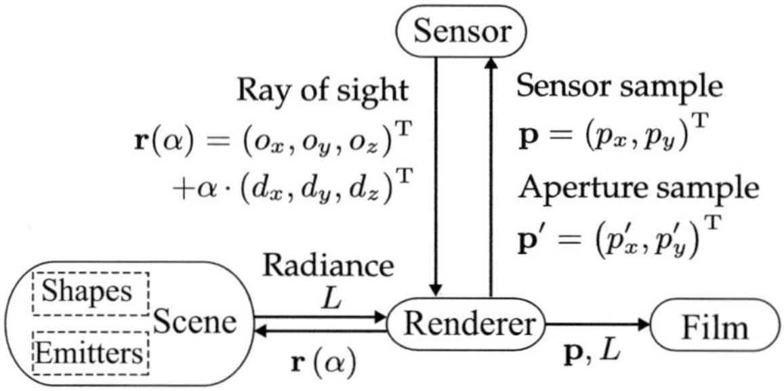

Figure 3.1: The core components of the Mitsuba renderer and how they interact with each other.

4 MC ViSi framework extensions

This section describes some of the major extensions to the Mitsuba renderer that are currently included in the MC ViSi framework.

4.1 Light sources

As mentioned in Sec. 3, a Mitsuba light source component has to provide one functionality: for a given intersection $\mathbf{q}_i$ of a traced ray of sight and the light source and the corresponding direction of incidence $\mathbf{q}_d$, there has to be a function that calculates the resulting spectrum of the emitted light. The following sections describe all the light sources contained in the proposed framework and explain how the spectra are calculated for a given query from the renderer.

4.1.1 Parallel emitter

The parallel emitter plugin realizes a telecentric light source. Such a light source emits light only into directions inside a cone having a certain angle β with respect to the surface normal $\mathbf{q}_n$ at the queried intersection $\mathbf{q}_i$ (see Fig. 4.1). The plugin has to be attached to an arbitrary shape (i.e., a geometric object) that provides the surface information. If the angle between the query direction $\mathbf{q}_d$ and the surface normal $\mathbf{q}_n$ is greater than β, a spectrum with all elements set to zero is returned—otherwise, the specified spectrum is returned.

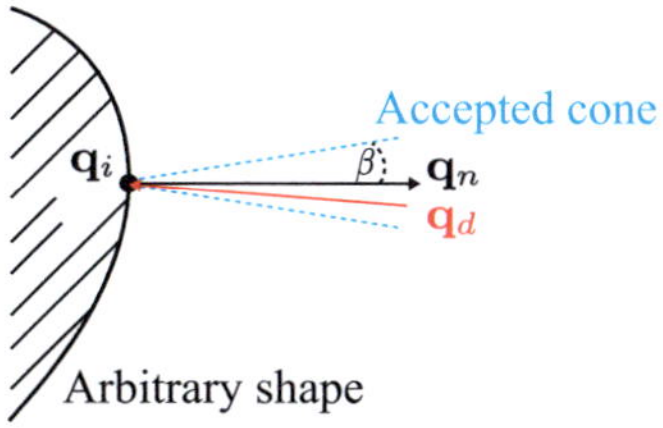

Figure 4.1: Schematic concept of the parallel emitter plugin: the red arrow denotes the queried direction $\mathbf{q}_d$ and $\mathbf{q}_n$ represents the surface normal at the queried surface point $\mathbf{q}_i$. Since the angle between $\mathbf{q}_d$ and $\mathbf{q}_n$ is less than the angle β of the accepted cone, light is emitted in the queried direction.

4.1.2 Telecentric projector

The telecentric projector plugin allows to simulate a spatially programmable area light source that consists of single pixels of the same size all emitting individual spectra. Figure 4.2 shows the principal setup of the plugin. The spectra can be conveniently defined by the user by providing an RGB image. The plugin has to be attached to a rectangular shape that determines the projector's overall size, position and orientation in the simulated scene. Similar to the parallel emitter plugin mentioned in the previous section, the pixels of the telecentric projector plugin emit light only inside a definable cone angle.

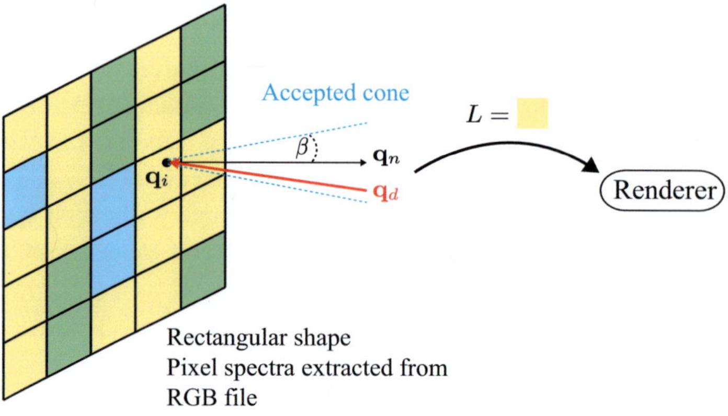

Figure 4.2: Schematic concept of the telecentric projector plugin: similar to the parallel emitter, every pixel of the simulated programmable area light source emits light inside a definable cone only. Since in the shown case the queried surface position lies inside a yellow pixel of the light source, the respective spectrum is returned to the renderer.

4.1.3 Light field emitter

Basically, the light field emitter extends the telecentric projector by also allowing to define individual spectra for different emission directions. By this means, the emission of a four dimensional light field can be simulated. This plugin is also attached to a rectangular 3D shape and also requires a an RGB image that provides the information about the emitted spectra. Additional parameters specify the light field emitter's spatial and angular resolution. The light field information is spatially multiplexed in the the RGB image as shown in Fig. 4.3.

For a given query by the renderer, at first the emitter's corresponding macro pixel is determined. Then, the intersection $\mathbf{i}$ of a virtual ray originating in the query direction from the origin $\mathbf{o}$ of the found macro pixel with a hemisphere of radius 1 located underneath the emitter plane is calculated. The position $\mathbf{i}$ is then projected on the emitter plane and the relative coordinates with respect to $\mathbf{o}$ allow to determine the angular component of the query, i.e., the actual spectrum to be read from the RGB image and to be returned to the renderer. This concept is visualized in Fig. 4.4.

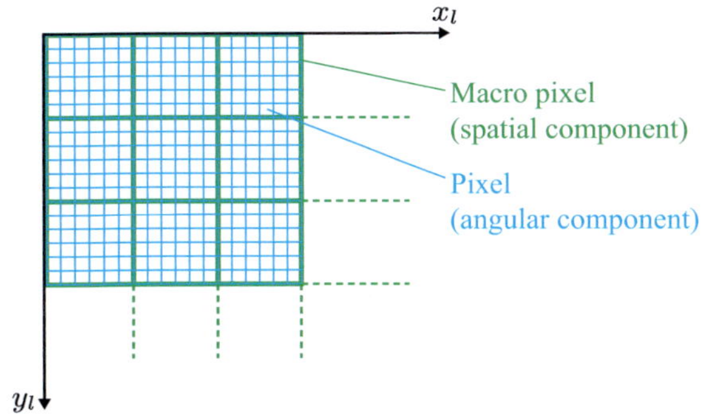

Figure 4.3: Spatial multiplexing of the light field emitter plugin for representing the spatial and angular component of the light field data in a two-dimensional RGB file. Single pixels are divided into macro pixels according to the specified angular resolution. The macro pixels carry the spatial component of the light field data and the underlying pixels represent the light field's angular component.

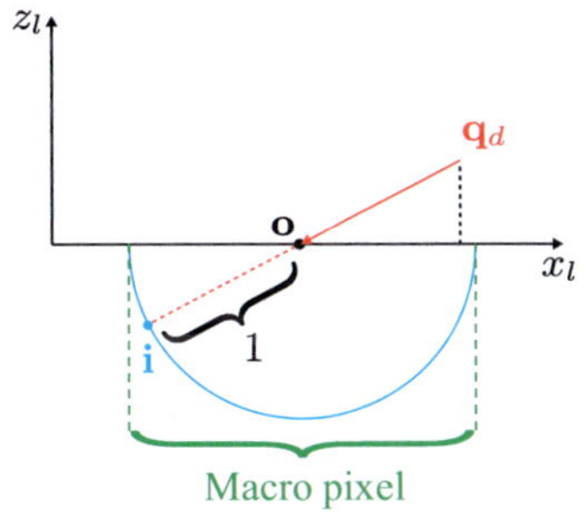

Figure 4.4: Schematic concept of the light field emitter: $\mathbf{o}$ denotes the center of the macro pixel, i.e., the spatial component of the light field data corresponding to the queried surface position and direction. The intersection $\mathbf{i}$ of the ray originating from $\mathbf{o}$ in direction $\mathbf{q}_d$ allows to obtain the correct pixel inside the determined macro pixel and to finally return the respective spectrum.

4.2 Sensors

Besides the described light source plugins, the MC ViSi framework also adds sensor plugins to the Mitsuba renderer. A sensor plugin has to provide a function that calculates the parameters of the ray of sight $\mathbf{r}(\alpha)$ corresponding to a pixel sample $\mathbf{p} = (p_x, p_y)^\mathrm{T}$ and—if applicable—an aperture sample $\mathbf{p}' = (p'_x, p'_y)^\mathrm{T}$. The following Sections are dedicated to MC ViSi's major sensor plugins and provide details about the respective steps needed to calculate the ray of sight.

4.2.1 Telecentric camera

Although Mitsuba already has a telecentric camera plugin, MC ViSi introduces its own implementation that uses types of parameters that are more common in the field of industrial machine vision. The provided plugin is based on a simple model of a telecentric camera as shown in Fig. 4.5. The required parameters are the sensor's focal length f, the image plane distance b, the pixel dimensions $\mathbf{l} = (l_x, l_y)$, the diameter D_t of the telecentric stop, the diameter D_l of the main lens and the number of pixels (M, N) in x- and y-direction.

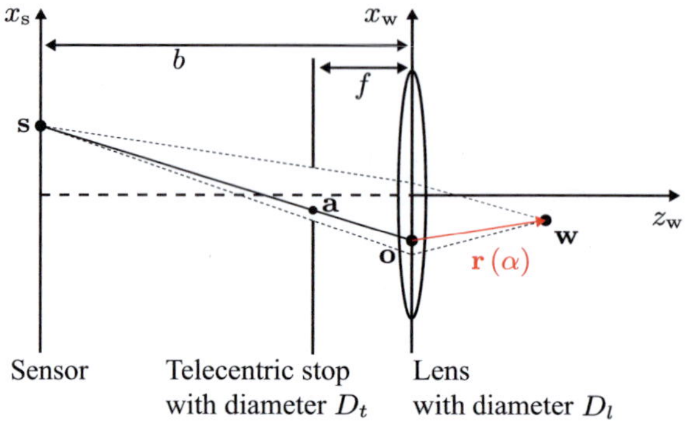

Figure 4.5: Schematic concept of the telecentric camera: visualization of the calculation of the ray of sight $\mathbf{r}(\alpha)$ corresponding to the position $\mathbf{s}$ on the sensor plane and the position $\mathbf{a}$ on the aperture plane.

For a given pixel sample $\mathbf{p}$ and an aperture sample $\mathbf{p}'$, the corresponding ray of sight $\mathbf{r}(\alpha)$ is calculated as follows: the samples $\mathbf{p}$ and $\mathbf{p}'$ are mapped to the respective positions $\mathbf{s} = (s_x, s_y)$ on the sensor plane and $\mathbf{a} = (a_x, a_y)^\mathrm{T}$ on the plane of the telecentric stop (i.e., the aperture plane) respectively. The intersection $\mathbf{o}$ of a ray running through $\mathbf{s}$ and $\mathbf{a}$ with the plane of the main lens denotes the origin of the ray of sight. If $\mathbf{o}$ lies outside the main lens, the spectrum corresponding to the respective ray of sight will be weighted with zero. The focused world point $\mathbf{w} = (w_x, w_y, w_z)^{\mathrm{T}}$ can be calculated by means of the thin lens formula [BLF15]:

$$\frac{1}{f} = \frac{1}{w_z} + \frac{1}{b} \Leftrightarrow \left(\frac{1}{f} - \frac{1}{b}\right) \tag{4.1}$$

and the intercept theorem

$$\begin{pmatrix} w_x \\ w_y \end{pmatrix} = -\frac{1}{b} \begin{pmatrix} w_z s_x \\ w_z s_y \end{pmatrix} . \tag{4.2}$$

The direction $\mathbf{d} = (d_x, d_y, d_z)^{\mathrm{T}}$ of the ray of sight can be obtained via

$$\mathbf{d} = \mathbf{w} - \mathbf{o} .$$

The presented implementation also covers depth of field effect as it accounts for the size of the sensor elements and for the aperture diameter.

4.2.2 Light field camera

A light field camera is able to not only resolve the (x, y)-position of captured light bundles but also their two-dimensional direction of incidence (θ, φ). By most commercially available light field cameras this is achieved by replacing the sensor by a micro lens array and by placing the actual sensor behind the micro lens array. The single elements of the micro lens array represent the system's spatial component. The micro lenses realize a mapping between the direction of the incoming light bundles and the sensor pixels that are located behind the respective micro lens. The set of pixels that correspond to one micro lens is usually called a macro pixel.

A light field camera of the described kind is modeled by the respective plugin of the MC ViSi framework. The plugin's parameters are the focal length f of the main lens, the image plane distance b, the diameter of the main lens D_l, the spatial resolution (M, N), the angular resolution (J, K) and the pixel dimensions $\mathbf{l} = (l_x, l_y)$.

In order to reduce the overall number of parameters, a more simplified light field camera model is used (see Fig. 4.6). In order to obtain the ray of sight $\mathbf{r}(\alpha)$

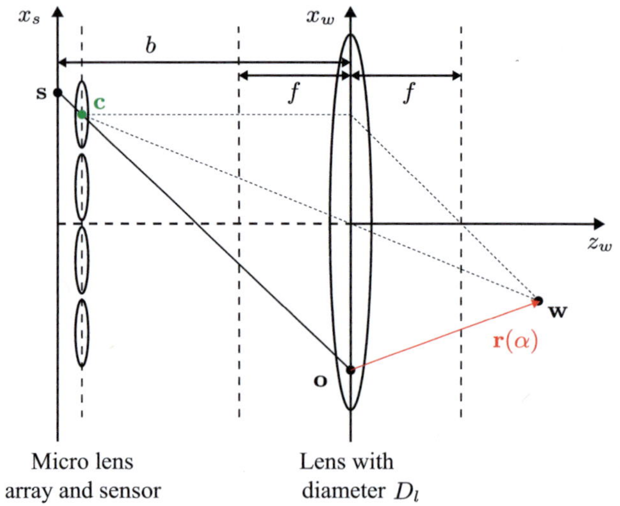

Figure 4.6: Schematic concept of the light field camera: visualization of the calculation of the ray of sight $\mathbf{r}(\alpha)$ corresponding to the position s on the sensor plane and thc center position $\mathbf{c}$ of the respective micro lens.

corresponding to a continuous pixel sample $\mathbf{p}$, at first the center $\mathbf{c} = (c_x, c_y)^{\mathrm{T}}$ of the respective micro lens, i.e., the macro pixel is determined, to which $\mathbf{p}$ belongs. The focused world point $\mathbf{w} = (w_x, w_y, w_z)^{\mathrm{T}}$ is calculated via the thin lens formula (4.1) and the intercept theorem (4.2) modified as

$$\begin{pmatrix} w_x \\ w_y \end{pmatrix} = -\frac{1}{b} \begin{pmatrix} w_z c_x \\ w_z c_y \end{pmatrix} .$$

All pixel positions of the same macro pixel are assumed to share the same focused world point $\mathbf{w}$, but to look at it from different directions. In the employed simplified model, the relative position of the pixel sample $\mathbf{p}$ with respect to its macro pixel is linearly mapped to the corresponding position $\mathbf{o}$ on the main lens:

$$\begin{pmatrix} o_x \\ o_y \\ o_z \end{pmatrix} = \begin{pmatrix} [1.8] - \left(\frac{p_x \bmod J}{J} \cdot 2 - 1 \right) \cdot \frac{D}{2} \\ - \left(\frac{p_y \bmod K}{K} \cdot 2 - 1 \right) \cdot \frac{D}{2} \\ 0 \end{pmatrix} .$$

Finally, the ray of sight is given by

$$\mathbf{r}(\alpha) = \mathbf{o} + \alpha \cdot (\mathbf{w} - \mathbf{o})\,.$$

5 Experiments

This section provides an example showing how two of the introduced plugins can be employed to simulate a novel machine vision system for the visual inspection of transparent objects as proposed in [MLB16b]. The system's principle optical setup is shown in Fig. 5.1. The parallel emitter plugin (see Sec. 4.1.1) can be used to simulate the collimated illumination and the light field camera plugin (see Sec. 4.2.2) allows to simulate the employed sensor. The described scene has been simulated for a defect-free test object instance and for a test object affected by a scattering material defect, i.e., an enclosed air bubble. In order to visually enhance material defects present inside the test objects, the authors propose the calculation of a special kind of image gradient that is based on the so-called Earth Mover's distance [RTG98] and that is suitable for light field images. Figure 5.2 shows the resulting gradient images visualized in pseudo colors.

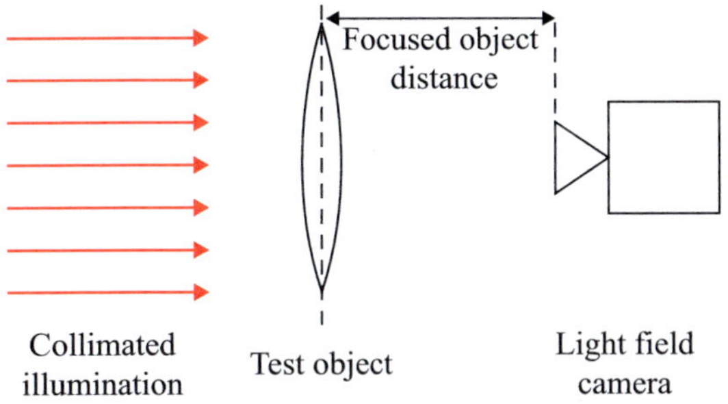

Figure 5.1: Optical setup of the simulated machine vision system: parallel light beams illuminate the test object, a double-convex lens, and a light field camera serves as the sensor.

Since the simulated experiments showed promising results for the method proposed in [MLB16b], the authors are currently setting up a real prototype for conducting further experiments.

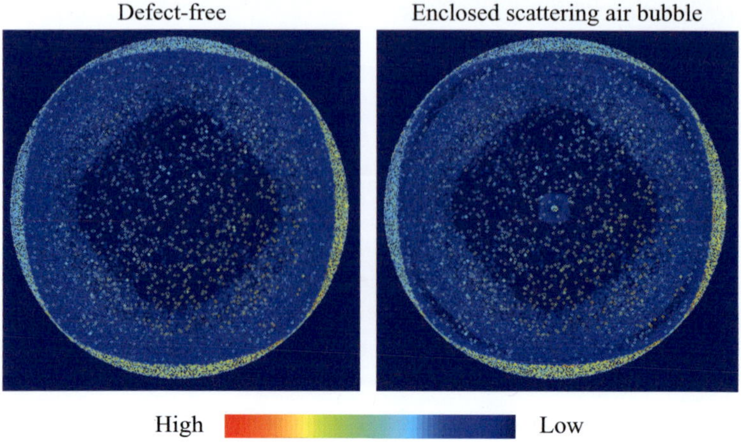

Figure 5.2: Pseudo color visualization of the output of the image gradient method based on the Earth Mover's distance applied to the light field images resulting from the simulation. In the right-hand side image, the scattering defect present in the test object's center is clearly visible.

6 Conclusion

This article introduced the machine vision simulation framework MC ViSi. The framework consists of several plugins that extend the physically based rendering software Mitsuba. Some of the proposed framework's main components, i.e., the parallel emitter, the telecentric projector, the light field emitter, the telecentric camera and the light field camera have been explained in detail. Furthermore, an example has been provided, where the introduced plugins have been employed in a simulation of a machine vision system for the inspection of transparent objects.

As future steps, the authors plan to extend the framework by further components, e.g., a plugin allowing to model retroreflective object surfaces and a sensor plugin modeling a laser scanner sensor.

Bibliography

[BLF15] Jürgen Beyerer, Fernando Puente León, and Christian Frese. *Machine Vision - Automated Visual Inspection: Theory, Practice and Applications*. Springer Berlin Heidelberg, 2015.

[BM+16] Stephan Bergmann, Mahsa Mohammadikaji, , Stephan Irgenfried, Heinz Wörn, Jürgen Beyerer, and Carsten Dachsbacher. A phenomenological approach to integrating gaussian beam properties and speckle into a physically-based renderer. In Matthias Hullin, Marc Stamminger, and Tino Weinkauf, editors, *Vision, Modeling Visualization*. The Eurographics Association, 2016.

[IDW14] Stephan Irgenfried, Frank Dittrich, and Heinz Wörn. Realization and evaluation of image processing tasks based on synthetic sensor data: 2 use cases. In *Forum Bildverarbeitung 2014*, pages 35–46, 2014.

[ITW11] Stephan Irgenfried, Igor Tchouchenkov, and Heinz Wörn. CADaVISION: A simulation framework for machine vision prototyping. In *Proceedings of the 2nd International Conference on Computer Modelling and Simulation CSSim 2011*, pages 59–67, 2011.

[Jak10] Wenzel Jakob. Mitsuba renderer, 2010. http://www.mitsuba-renderer.org.

[MBI+16] Mahsa Mohammadikaji, Stephan Bergmann, Stephan Irgenfried, Jürgen Beyerer, Carsten Dachsbacher, and Heinz Wörn. A framework for uncertainty propagation in 3d shape measurement using laser triangulation. In *2016 IEEE International Instrumentation and Measurement Technology Conference Proceedings*, pages 1–6, 2016.

[MGLB16] Johannes Meyer, Robin Gruna, Thomas Längle, and Jürgen Beyerer. Simulation of an inverse schlieren image acquisition system for inspecting transparent objects. *Electronic Imaging*, 2016(19):1–9, 2016.

[MLB16a] Johannes Meyer, Thomas Längle, and Jürgen Beyerer. About acquiring and processing light transport matrices for transparent object inspection. *tm-Technisches Messen*, 2016.

[MLB16b] Johannes Meyer, Thomas Längle, and Jürgen Beyerer. About the acquisition and processing of ray deflection histograms for transparent object inspection. In *Irish Machine Vision and Image Processing Conference*, pages 9–16. Irish Pattern Recognition and Classification Society, 2016.

[MLB16c] Johannes Meyer, Thomas Längle, and Jürgen Beyerer. Acquisition and processing of light transport matrices for automated transparent object inspection. In *Forum Bildverarbeitung 2016*, pages 75–86, 2016.

[NZL16] Thomas Nürnberg, Christian Zimmermann, and Fernando Puente León. Simulationsgestützte Optimierung einer Computational-Kamera zur dichten Tiefenschätzung. *tm - Technisches Messen*, 83(9), January 2016.

[RTG98] Yossi Rubner, Carlo Tomasi, and Leonidas Guibas. A metric for distributions with applications to image databases. In *Computer Vision, 1998. Sixth International Conference on*, pages 59–66. IEEE, 1998.

Different Designs for a Polarization State Detector Based on Division-of-Amplitude

Christian Negara

Fraunhofer Institute of Optronics,
System Technologies and Image Exploitation IOSB
Fraunhoferstr. 1, 76131 Karlsruhe, Germany
christian.negara@iosb.fraunhofer.de

Technical Report IES-2016-07

Abstract: A polarization state detector (PSD) measures all parameters of the state of polarization of the detected light. The state of polarization is described by four Stokes parameters while the total phase of the light is discarded. Only four intensity measurements are needed to measure the four Stokes parameters even though the Stokes vector is defined by six intensity measurements. By using a special optical design with four photodetectors, these measurements can be conducted simultaneously. To measure the Stokes vector with high accuracy, a special beam splitter has been proposed in the literature imposing constraints on the reflectance, transmittance and retardance of the p- and s-polarized reflected and transmitted wave. Later on, several alternative designs have been proposed using two or more retarders and ordinary beam splitters. In this report another alternative design of the PSD is presented. In fact, only two instead of four waveplates are needed to get optimal results for ordinary beam splitters with suboptimal optical properties.

1 Introduction

For the characterization of surfaces and layered structures, the polarization of light often carries out important information. One measurement technique using the polarization of light is called ellipsometry. This technique can be used for measuring the thickness of coated surfaces or the optical constants of materials like the index of refraction or the extinction coefficient. When measuring the thickness of a layer, this technique is very sensitive to thickness variations and can even detect changes of a monolayer or incompleted monolayers. The setup typically consists of a light source which emits polarized light and a detector consisting of a PSD which detects the state of polarization of the incoming light. The emitted light is reflected or transmitted at the sample under study. The state of polarization of the reflected or transmitted light is changed according to the material properties of the sample. To achieve a high sensitivity to e.g. thickness variations, the PSD must precisely detect the state of polarization. A PSD called division-of-amplitude photopolarimeter (DOAP) without any moving parts like rotating quarter-wave plates has been proposed in [Azz82]. This PSD splits up the the incoming light ray into four rays with lower amplitude which are detected by four photodetectors. A key component of the DOAP is a beam splitter which fist splits up the incoming light into two rays, the reflected and transmitted light path. This first beam splitter can be characterized by six optical parameters, three for the reflected and three for the transmitted light path. The optical parameters of this beam splitter are critical, since they have an influence on the uncertainty of measurement of the state of polarization described by the Stokes vector and calculated by the measured intensities. In [AD03] optimal values for the optical parameters of the beam splitter have been provided to get a low sensitivity to measurement errors [JCG08]. A beam splitter for which the six optical parameters are optimal, can be quite complex.

As has been shown in previous work, it is also possible to get optimal values for the sensitivity coefficients if only four of the six optical parameters of the beam splitter are optimal. This is achieved by adding retarders to the DOAP. The generalized design of the DOAP is shown in Figure 1.1. The retarders are optional and only needed if the optical parameters of the beam splitter BS_i are suboptimal. There are two kinds of beam splitters in the DOAP. The most critical component of the DOAP is the beam splitter BS_i, which has to be properly designed to be able to measure light with an arbitrary state of polarization. E.g. the change of polarization on the reflected or transmitted path must differ, hence unpolarizing beam splitters are not suitable. The beam splitters BS_r and BS_t split up the state of polarization of the incoming light wave into two orthogonal linearly polarized waves. BS_r and BS_t could be e.g. Rochon prisms, Wollaston prisms, Nomarski prisms or polarizing beam splitters like cubes or plates.

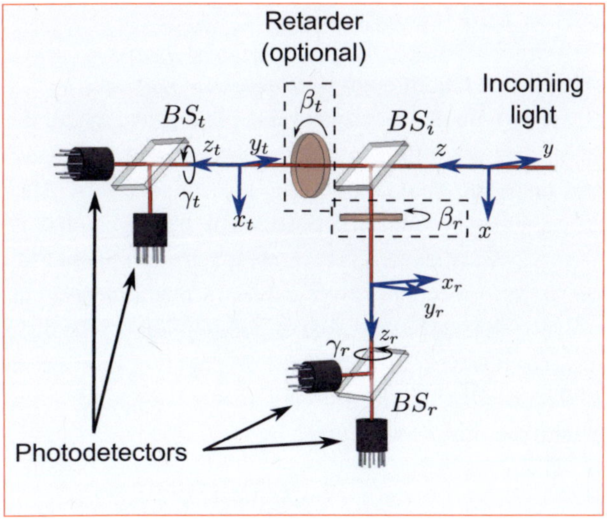

Figure 1.1: Scheme of the DOAP.

In [ZCTH17] several different designs have been examined using quarter and half wave plates on the transmitted or reflected light path to improve the sensitivity of the DOAP while a suboptimal beam splitter BS_i was used. Although the retarders improve the sensitivity, no comparison has been made to the optimal design of the DOAP provided in [AD03]. In our previous work [Neg16] another design of the DOAP based on quarter-wave plates has been studied and compared with the optimal design. The DOAP presented there contains four quarter-wave plates, two on the reflected and transmitted path, respectively. It has been shown empirically that four quarter-wave plates are sufficient to compensate the negative effect of a suboptimal beam splitter on the sensitivity coefficients. By adjusting the rotational angles of the retarders, the absolute value of the sensitivity coefficients can be lowered. In the present work it is shown that not four but only two quarter-wave plates are needed to get an optimal DOAP.

1.1 Reflection and transmission

Usually, a light ray traveling through isotropic, homogeneous and non-absorbing media is locally approximated by a transverse plane wave where the electric and magnetic field vectors are orthogonal to the direction of propagation. Because the electric and magnetic field components are connected by Maxwell's equations, the light wave can be fully described solely by the electric field. Because there are two linearly independent vectors which are orthogonal to the direction of propagation, transverse plane waves exhibit a phenomenon called polarization. A light wave with an arbitrary state of polarization can be decomposed into two linearly polarized waves. A light wave propagating in z direction is shown in Figure 1.2. The oscillating electric field vector is dependent on the position $\boldsymbol{x} = (x, y, z)^\mathsf{T}$ and the time t and is given by

$$\underline{\boldsymbol{E}}(\boldsymbol{x}, t) = \begin{pmatrix} \underline{E}_x(\boldsymbol{x}, t) \\ \underline{E}_y(\boldsymbol{x}, t) \\ 0 \end{pmatrix}$$

where $\underline{E}_x(\boldsymbol{x}, t)$ and $\underline{E}_y(\boldsymbol{x}, t)$ are the oscillating electric field vectors of the two linearly polarized waves in x and y direction, respectively. The x-, y- and z-axis form a right-handed coordinate system, where the z-axis is the direction of propagation. For coherent light, which will be the main focus in the rest of the paper, the linearly polarized waves $\underline{E}_x$ and $\underline{E}_y$ can be written as:

$$\begin{aligned} \underline{E}_x(\boldsymbol{x}, t) &= \underline{E}_{0x} \cdot \mathrm{e}^{\,\mathrm{i}(k_z z - \omega t)}, \\ \underline{E}_y(\boldsymbol{x}, t) &= \underline{E}_{0y} \cdot \mathrm{e}^{\,\mathrm{i}(k_z z - \omega t)}. \end{aligned}$$

where $\underline{E}_{0x}$ and $\underline{E}_{0y}$ are the complex amplitudes, k_z is the circular wavenumber and ω the angular frequency. The complex amplitudes can be written as

$$\underline{E}_{0x} = E_{0x} \cdot \mathrm{e}^{\,\mathrm{i}\varphi_x}, \qquad \underline{E}_{0y} = E_{0y} \cdot \mathrm{e}^{\,\mathrm{i}\varphi_y} \tag{1.1}$$

with the (real) amplitudes E_{0x} and E_{0y} and the initial phases φ_x and φ_y. When the light wave impinges on the plane surface between two homogeneous media it is partly reflected and partly refracted. If the incident light ray hits the surface under an oblique angle of incidence, the so-called plane of incidence is being spanned through two vectors, the direction of propagation of the incident light wave and the surface normal. In isotropic media the vectors for the direction of

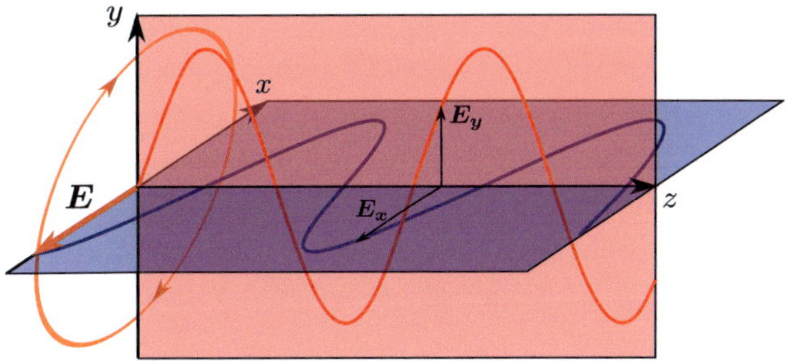

Figure 1.2: Decomposition of an elliptically polarized light wave into two linearly polarized waves.

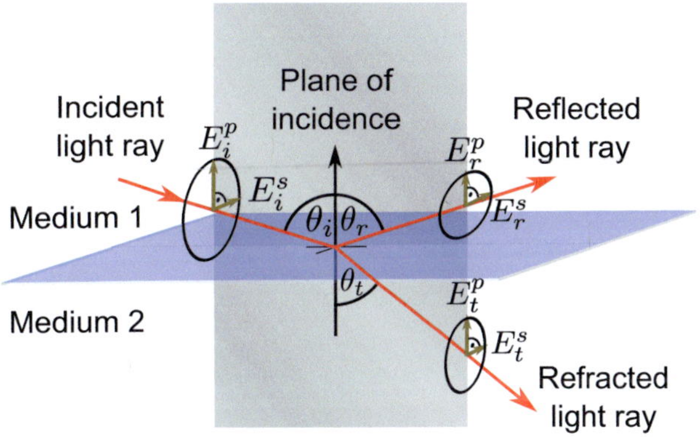

Figure 1.3: Reflection and refraction split up into p- and s-polarized waves.

propagation of the incident, reflected and refracted light waves all lie in the plane of incidence. The incident, reflected and refracted or transmitted wave can be decomposed into two linearly polarized light waves. Because the decomposition shown in Figure 1.2 is not unique, the x-axis can be aligned parallel and the y-axis perpendicular to the plane of incidence which is also the convention. The two linearly polarized light waves in x and y direction are then called p- and s-polarized, respectively. Equation (1.1) then becomes:

$$\underline{E}^p = E^p \cdot \mathrm{e}^{\,\mathrm{i}\varphi^p}, \qquad \underline{E}^s = E^s \cdot \mathrm{e}^{\,\mathrm{i}\varphi^s} \tag{1.2}$$

with the complex amplitudes $\underline{E}^p$ and $\underline{E}^s$, the real amplitudes E^p and E^s and the initial phases φ^p and φ^s. The decomposition of the incident, reflected and transmitted wave into p- and s-polarized waves is shown in Figure 1.3. The amplitudes and the initial phases from Equation (1.2) are denoted with the subscript i for the incident, r for the reflected and t for the transmitted wave. With this definition, the change of the state of polarization resulting from reflection can be described by two reflection coefficients $\underline{r}^p$ and $\underline{r}^s$, which are generally complex:

$$\underline{r}^p = \frac{\underline{E}_r^p}{\underline{E}_i^p}, \qquad \underline{r}^s = \frac{\underline{E}_r^s}{\underline{E}_i^s}\,. \tag{1.3}$$

The change of the state of polarization resulting from refraction can be described by the transmission coefficients $\underline{t}^p$ and $\underline{t}^s$:

$$\underline{t}^p = \frac{\underline{E}_t^p}{\underline{E}_i^p}, \qquad \underline{t}^s = \frac{\underline{E}_t^s}{\underline{E}_i^s}\,. \tag{1.4}$$

At a single surface between two isotropic materials there is no energy flux from the p- to the s-polarized wave and vice versa when the light is reflected or refracted. From Equation (1.2), (1.3) and (1.4) we obtain for the real amplitudes $E_i^p, E_i^s, E_r^p, E_r^s, E_t^p$ and E_t^s of the incident, reflected and transmitted wave:

$$\begin{aligned} E_r^p &= |\underline{r}^p| \cdot E_i^p, \qquad & E_r^s &= |\underline{r}^s| \cdot E_i^s, \\ E_t^p &= |\underline{t}^p| \cdot E_i^p, \qquad & E_t^s &= |\underline{t}^s| \cdot E_i^s\,. \end{aligned}$$

Furthermore, $\underline{r}^p, \underline{r}^s, \underline{t}^p$ and $\underline{t}^s$ can not only be used to describe the change of the state of polarization at a single interface, but also at several interfaces of isotropic materials. This is possible as long as the surface normals of the interfaces all lie in a single plane of incidence. The light waves passing through an optical component on a reflected or transmitted path superimpose and contribute to the complex amplitude of the electric field of the reflected or transmitted light. As an example, the change of the state of polarization of a light ray on the reflected or transmitted light path of a beam splitter (see Figure 1.4 and Figure 1.5) can be described by the reflection and transmission coefficients $\underline{r}^p, \underline{r}^s, \underline{t}^p$ and $\underline{t}^s$. This is also true if the beam splitter consists of multiple layers or if it has anti-reflection coatings. In this case, the reflected or transmitted light usually undergoes several reflections and refractions.

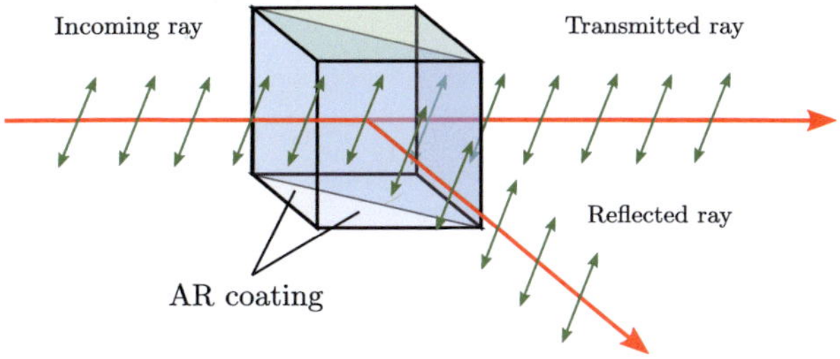

Figure 1.4: Reflected and transmitted light path at a non-polarizing beam splitter

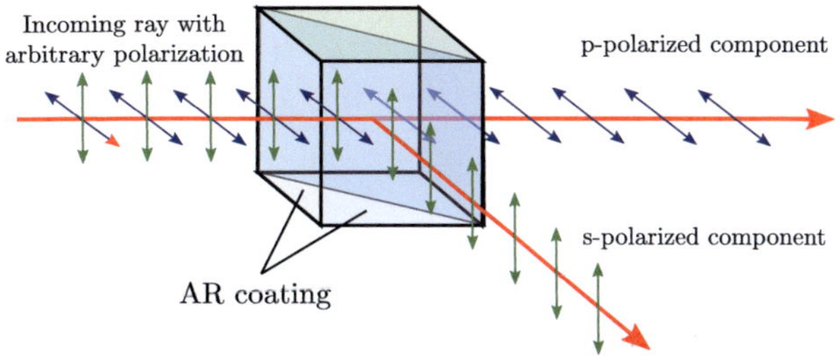

Figure 1.5: Reflected and transmitted light path at a polarizing beam splitter

Two important parameters in ellipsometry are Ψ and Δ. $\Psi \in [0°, 90°]$ describes the change of the amplitude quotient and $\Delta \in [0°, 360°]$ the change of the phase difference caused by reflection or transmission of two orthogonal linearly polarized waves. Ψ and Δ are related to the reflection coefficients by the fundamental equation of ellipsometry [TM99]:

$$\tan \Psi_r \cdot \mathrm{e}^{\,\mathrm{i}\Delta_r} = \frac{\underline{r}^p}{\underline{r}^s}$$

where the subscript r denotes that the parameters are assigned to the reflected wave. For the complex transmission coefficients with the subscript t, the parameters Ψ_t and Δ_t are defined in the same manner:

$$\tan \Psi_t \cdot \mathrm{e}^{\,\mathrm{i}\Delta_t} = \frac{\underline{t}^p}{\underline{t}^s} \, .$$

For describing the state of polarization of the reflected or transmitted light, the total phase of the wave is of no interest because it does not affect the shape of the polarization ellipse and the direction of rotation of the electric field. The shape of the polarization ellipse and the direction of rotation are fully determined by the (real) amplitudes E^p and E^s of the electric field and the phase difference $\varphi^p - \varphi^s$ of the initial phases. For the phase differences of the incident, reflected and transmitted wave we get

$$\begin{aligned} \arg(\underline{E}_r^p) &= \arg(\underline{r}^p) + \arg(\underline{E}_i^p), & \arg(\underline{E}_r^s) &= \arg(\underline{r}^s) + \arg(\underline{E}_i^s), \\ \arg(\underline{E}_t^p) &= \arg(\underline{t}^p) + \arg(\underline{E}_i^p), & \arg(\underline{E}_t^s) &= \arg(\underline{t}^s) + \arg(\underline{E}_i^s), \end{aligned}$$

and hence

$$\begin{aligned} \varphi_r^p - \varphi_r^s &= \underbrace{\arg(\underline{r}^p) - \arg(\underline{r}^s)}_{=\Delta_r} + \varphi_i^p - \varphi_i^s, \\ \varphi_t^p - \varphi_t^s &= \underbrace{\arg(\underline{t}^p) - \arg(\underline{t}^s)}_{=\Delta_t} + \varphi_i^p - \varphi_i^s \end{aligned} \tag{1.5}$$

where $\arg(x)$ returns the argument of a complex number x. Another quantity we will use is the intensity I of a light wave. The relationship between the intensity I and the amplitude of the electic field E of a light wave in non-magnetic and non-absorbing material is given by [BPLF16]:

$$I = \frac{1}{2}\varepsilon_0 c_0 n E^2 \tag{1.6}$$

where c_0 is the speed of light in vacuum, ε_0 the vacuum permittivity, n the real index of refraction of the material and $E^2 = E_{0x}^2 + E_{0y}^2$. To measure the intensity in an absorbing medium with complex index of refraction $\underline{n}$, the formula in Equation (1.6) becomes more complex because the direction of the Poynting vector generally exhibits an elliptical oscillation [DAP94b]. The intensity is the power of the electro-magnetic field per unit area. When measuring the intensity of an electro-magnetic plane wave, the power is measured on an area which is orthogonal to the direction of propagation.

For describing amplitude ratios of the incident and reflected or transmitted wave, the complex coefficients $\underline{r}^p$ and $\underline{r}^s$, $\underline{t}^p$ and $\underline{t}^s$ are used. Similarly, intensity ratios of the incident, reflected and transmitted wave can be described by the reflectances R^p and R^s and the transmittances T^p and T^s. Let I_i^p and I_i^s be the intensities of the incident, I_r^p and I_r^s of the reflected and I_t^p and I_t^s of the transmitted p- and s-polarized waves. R^p, R^s, T^p and T^s are then given by:

$$\begin{aligned} R^p &= b_r \frac{I_r^p}{I_i^p} = b_r |\underline{r}^p|^2, \qquad & R^s &= b_r \frac{I_r^s}{I_i^s} = b_r |\underline{r}^s|^2, \\ T^p &= b_t \frac{I_t^p}{I_i^p} = b_t |\underline{t}^p|^2, \qquad & T^s &= b_t \frac{I_t^s}{I_i^s} = b_t |\underline{t}^s|^2 \end{aligned} \tag{1.7}$$

where b_r and b_t are proportionality constants resulting from the fact that the unit area for measuring the power of the incoming and reflected or transmitted wave is not measured orthogonal to the direction of propagation. Instead, the surface power density is measured on a unit area at the boundary surface between different media. A detailed explanation of how to compute b_r and b_t at an interface between two different media can be found in [Hec02]. It should be noted that the reflected path, e.g. through a beam splitter, can contain multiple reflections and transmissions through different media. Therefore, in contrast to reflection at a single interface, it is possible that $b_r \neq 1$.

The reflectances and transmittances R^p, R^s, T^p and T^s are related to Ψ_r and Ψ_t by:

$$\tan^2 \Psi_r = \frac{R^p}{R^s}, \qquad \tan^2 \Psi_t = \frac{T^p}{T^s} \,. \tag{1.8}$$

The reflectance R and transmittance T is defined as the intensity ratio of the incident to the reflected and transmitted wave, respectively. We will define R_u and T_u as the average value of the reflectances and transmittances of the p- and s-polarized waves [TM99]:

$$R_u = \frac{R^p + R^s}{2}, \qquad T_u = \frac{T^p + T^s}{2} \,. \tag{1.9}$$

For linearly polarized light at $45°$, circularly polarized and unpolarized light, we obtain: $R_u = R$ and $T_u = T$. This identity is not generally valid [Hec02]. In the absence of absorption, i.e. the refractive indices are real, we get:

$$R^s + T^s = R^p + T^p = 1 \,. \tag{1.10}$$

This equation is also valid for non-absorbing beam splitters with multiple reflections and transmissions.

Substituting Equation (1.8) into Equation (1.9) we get

$$\begin{aligned} R_u &= \frac{R^p}{2}\left(1+\tan^2\Psi_r\right) = \frac{R^s}{2}\left(\frac{1}{\tan^2\Psi_r}+1\right), \\ T_u &= \frac{T^p}{2}\left(1+\tan^2\Psi_t\right) = \frac{T^s}{2}\left(\frac{1}{\tan^2\Psi_t}+1\right). \end{aligned}$$

By solving for R^p, R^s, T^p and T^s we obtain

$$\begin{aligned} R^p &= 2R_u\frac{\tan^2\Psi_r}{1+\tan^2\Psi_r}, \qquad & R^s &= 2R_u\frac{1}{1+\tan^2\Psi_r}, \\ T^p &= 2T_u\frac{\tan^2\Psi_t}{1+\tan^2\Psi_t}, \qquad & T^s &= 2T_u\frac{1}{1+\tan^2\Psi_t}. \end{aligned} \tag{1.11}$$

In case that $b_r = b_t = 1$ we see from Equation (1.11) and Equation (1.7) that the change of the amplitudes of the reflected wave, which are determined by $|\underline{r}^p|$ and $|\underline{r}^s|$, can be described by Ψ_r and R_u. Hence, by using Equation (1.5) the change of the state of polarization resulting from reflection at an isotropic surface is fully determined by Ψ_r, Δ_r and R_u. The change of the state of polarization of the transmitted wave is determined by Ψ_t, Δ_t and T_u.

If $b_r \neq 1$ or $b_t \neq 1$ the change of the state of polarization can still be described by $\Psi_r, \Delta_r, R_u, \Psi_t, \Delta_t$ and T_u. In this case the only unknown is the size of the polarization ellipse of the electric field. This is due to the definition of the surface power density ratios in Equation (1.7). If the ratio would simply be the quotient of the intensities of the incoming and reflected or transmitted wave, the equation $R^p + T^p = R^s + T^s = 1$ would not be generally true anymore in the non-absorbing case. This is because $|r^p|^2 + |t^p|^2$ and $|r^s|^2 + |t^s|^2$can take values lower than 1.

If the beam spitter BS_i is non-absorbing i.e. Equation (1.10) is valid and if the beam splitter splits up the intensity equally on the reflected and transmitted path i.e. $R_u = T_u = 0.5$ we get from Equation (1.11) [AD03]:

$$\begin{aligned} T^s + R^s = 1 &= \frac{1}{1+\tan^2\Psi_t} + \frac{1}{1+\tan^2\Psi_r} \Leftrightarrow \\ \frac{\tan^2\Psi_t}{1+\tan^2\Psi_t} &= \frac{1}{1+\tan^2\Psi_r} \Leftrightarrow \\ \tan^2\Psi_t\tan^2\Psi_r &= 1 \Leftrightarrow \\ \Psi_t &= \frac{\pi}{2} - \Psi_r \,. \end{aligned} \tag{1.12}$$

Two beam splitters are usually of special interest. A non-polarizing beam splitter splits up the incoming ray into two rays while $R^p = R^s$ and $T^p = T^s$ as shown in Figure 1.4. In this case $\Psi_r = \Psi_t = 45°$. A polarizing beam splitter separates the p- and s-polarized components of the incident wave on the reflected and transmitted path as shown in Figure 1.5. In this case either $\Psi_r = 0°$ and $\Psi_t = 90°$ or $\Psi_r = 90°$ and $\Psi_t = 0°$.

1.2 Stokes-Mueller Calculus

One convenient way describing the state of polarization for totally, as well as partly polarized light, is by a four-dimensional Stokes vector $\boldsymbol{S} \in \mathbb{R}^4$. The Stokes vector of polarized light is referenced to a fixed right-handed coordinate system (x, y, z) and the z-axis points to the observer. The conventions about the coordinate systems and transformations used in this paper can be found in [HMS80]. The definition of the Stokes vector $\boldsymbol{S}$ is [Fuj07]:

$$\boldsymbol{S} = \begin{pmatrix} S_0 \\ S_1 \\ S_2 \\ S_3 \end{pmatrix} = \begin{pmatrix} I_{0°} + I_{90°} \\ I_{0°} - I_{90°} \\ I_{45°} - I_{-45°} \\ I_R - I_L \end{pmatrix}$$

where $I_{0°}, I_{90°}, I_{45°}$ and $I_{-45°}$ are the measured intensities of a light wave (see Equation (1.6)) after passing linear polarizers which are rotated at $0°, 90°, 45°$ and $-45°$, respectively. I_L and I_R are the measured intensities after it passes left and right circular polarizers. The intensity of the light wave according to Equation (1.6) is determined by the Stokes parameter S_0 and can be derived from the aforementioned intensities by the following identities:

$$S_0 = I_{0°} + I_{90°} = I_{45°} + I_{-45°} = I_L + I_R \,.$$

The transformation of a Stokes vector resulting from interaction of light with an optical element can be described by the so-called Mueller matrix $\mathbf{M} \in \mathbb{R}^{4\times4}$. Let $\boldsymbol{S}^{in}$ be the Stokes vector of a light ray before and $\boldsymbol{S}^{out}$ after the state of polarization is changed by an optical component with Mueller matrix $\mathbf{M}$. We obtain:

$$\boldsymbol{S}^{out} = \mathbf{M} \cdot \boldsymbol{S}^{in} \,. \tag{1.13}$$

If the optical component with Mueller matrix $\mathbf{M}$ consists of several successive components with Mueller matrices $\mathbf{M}_1, \ldots, \mathbf{M}_n$, Equation (1.13) becomes

$$\boldsymbol{S}^{out} = \underbrace{\mathbf{M}_n \cdot \mathbf{M}_{n-1} \cdot \ldots \cdot \mathbf{M}_1}_{=:\mathbf{M}} \cdot \boldsymbol{S}^{in} .$$

If the light ray with the Stokes vector $\boldsymbol{S}^{out}$ hits a photodetector which is insensitive to the state of polarization, only the intensity S_0^{out} of the Stokes vector $\boldsymbol{S}^{out}$ is measured. The measured intensity S_0^{out} can be computed by:

$$S_0^{out} = \boldsymbol{q} \cdot \mathbf{M} \cdot \boldsymbol{S}^{in}$$

with $\boldsymbol{q} = (1, 0, 0, 0)$. $\boldsymbol{q} \cdot \mathbf{M}$ is then the first row of $\mathbf{M}$.

For a Mueller matrix $\mathbf{M}$ of an optical component which is referenced by a right-handed coordinate system with axes x, y and z, where z is the direction of propagation of the light wave, the Mueller matrix of an optical component rotated around the z-axis at an angle α is given by [Fuj07]:

$$\mathbf{R}(-\alpha) \cdot \mathbf{M} \cdot \mathbf{R}(\alpha) \tag{1.14}$$

where

$$\mathbf{R}(\alpha) = \begin{pmatrix} 1 & 0 & 0 & 0 \\ 0 & \cos 2\alpha & \sin 2\alpha & 0 \\ 0 & -\sin 2\alpha & \cos 2\alpha & 0 \\ 0 & 0 & 0 & 1 \end{pmatrix} .$$

If the change of the state of polarization on the reflected light path of a beam-splitter is described by the parameters Ψ_r, Δ_r and R_u, the corresponding Mueller matrix can be calculated by the following formula:

$$\mathbf{M}_S(\Psi_r, \Delta_r, R_u) =$$
$$R_u \begin{pmatrix} 1 & -\cos 2\Psi_r & 0 & 0 \\ -\cos 2\Psi_r & 1 & 0 & 0 \\ 0 & 0 & \sin 2\Psi_r \cos \Delta_r & \sin 2\Psi_r \sin \Delta_r \\ 0 & 0 & -\sin 2\Psi_r \sin \Delta_r & \sin 2\Psi_r \cos \Delta_r \end{pmatrix}$$

where the coordinate system for the Stokes vector of the incoming light ray is referenced to the plane of incidence of the beam splitter. Similarly, the Mueller matrix for the transmitted path is given by $\mathbf{M}_S(\Psi_t, \Delta_t, T_u)$. The Mueller matrix of a polarizer with the transmission axis rotated at 0°, which corresponds to the x-axis, is given by:

$$\mathbf{M}_P(0^\circ) = \frac{1}{2}\begin{pmatrix} 1 & 1 & 0 & 0 \\ 1 & 1 & 0 & 0 \\ 0 & 0 & 0 & 0 \\ 0 & 0 & 0 & 0 \end{pmatrix} .$$

The Mueller matrix of a polarizer rotated at an arbitrary angle α around the z-axis can be computed by Equation (1.14) and is denoted as $\mathbf{M}_P(\alpha)$. The Mueller matrix of a retarder with retardation δ where the fast axis points to the x-axis is given by:

$$\mathbf{M}_\Delta(\delta, 0^\circ) = \begin{pmatrix} 1 & 0 & 0 & 0 \\ 0 & 1 & 0 & 0 \\ 0 & 0 & \cos(\delta) & \sin(\delta) \\ 0 & 0 & -\sin(\delta) & \cos(\delta) \end{pmatrix} .$$

The Mueller matrix $\mathbf{M}_\Delta(\delta, \alpha)$ of a retarder with retardation δ which is rotated around the z-axis can be calculated again by using Equation (1.14). Because quarter-wave plates are retarders of special interest with $\delta = 90^\circ$, we will denote quarter-wave plates rotated by α as $\mathbf{M}_Q(\alpha) = \mathbf{M}_\Delta(90^\circ, \alpha)$.

2 DOAP without Retarders

In the previous section we described the mathematical formulation for the state of polarization and its change resulting from one or several optical components. We can now derive the Mueller matrix for one light path of the DOAP from Figure 1.1 without retarders. The polarizing beam splitters BS_r and BS_t are rotated at 45° ($\gamma_r = \gamma_t = 45^\circ$). The Mueller matrix for a light ray which is reflected at the beam splitter BS_i and then impinges on a polarizing beam splitter with the transmission axis at 45° is given by:

$$\mathbf{M}_P(45^\circ) \cdot \mathbf{M}_S(\Psi_r, \Delta_r, R_u) .$$

Let I_0 be the intensity measured by a polarization-insensitive photo-detector for the previously described light path and let $\boldsymbol{S}_i$ be the Stokes vector of the incoming light. We then get the following relationship:

$$I_0 = \boldsymbol{q} \cdot \mathbf{M}_P(45^\circ) \cdot \mathbf{M}_S(\Psi_r, \Delta_r, R_u) \cdot \boldsymbol{S}_i \; .$$

By computing the Mueller matrices for all four light paths we obtain a mapping from the Stokes vector $\boldsymbol{S}_i$ to the four intensity measurements I_0, I_1, I_2 and I_3:

$$\boldsymbol{I} := \begin{pmatrix} I_0 \\ I_1 \\ I_2 \\ I_3 \end{pmatrix} = \underbrace{\begin{pmatrix} \boldsymbol{q} \cdot \mathbf{M}_P(45^\circ) & \cdot \mathbf{M}_S(\Psi_r, \Delta_r, R_u) \\ \boldsymbol{q} \cdot \mathbf{M}_P(-45^\circ) & \cdot \mathbf{M}_S(\Psi_r, \Delta_r, R_u) \\ \boldsymbol{q} \cdot \mathbf{M}_P(45^\circ) & \cdot \mathbf{M}_S(\Psi_t, \Delta_t, T_u) \\ \boldsymbol{q} \cdot \mathbf{M}_P(-45^\circ) & \cdot \mathbf{M}_S(\Psi_t, \Delta_t, T_u) \end{pmatrix}}_{=:\mathbf{A}} \cdot \boldsymbol{S}_i \tag{2.1}$$

where $\mathbf{A} \in \mathbb{R}^{4\times 4}$ is called the instrument matrix of the PSD. By measuring the intensity vector $\boldsymbol{I}$, the incoming Stokes vector $\boldsymbol{S}_i$ can be calculated by

$$\boldsymbol{S}_i = \mathbf{A}^{-1} \cdot \boldsymbol{I}$$

if the instrument matrix is non-singular. To design an optimal DOAP, the optical parameters $\Psi_r, \Delta_r, R_u, \Psi_t, \Delta_t$ and T_u of the beam splitter BS_i must be chosen in such a way that we get optimal values for the sensitivity coefficients given by $\mathbf{A}^{-1}$. One possibility to minimize the absolute value of the sensitivity coefficients is to minimize $|\det \mathbf{A}^{-1}|$ which corresponds to the maximum of $|\det \mathbf{A}|$. We will denote the instrument matrix of the design of the DOAP (see Equation (2.1)) without any retarders as $\mathbf{A}_{\text{DOAP}}$. The optimal optical parameters of the beam splitter BS_i are given by [AD03]:

$$R_u^* = T_u^* = 0.5, \tag{2.2}$$
$$\Delta_r^* - \Delta_t^* = \pm 90^\circ, \tag{2.3}$$
$$\Psi_r^* = \frac{1}{2} \arccos(\pm 1/\sqrt{3}), \tag{2.4}$$
$$\Psi_t^* = 90^\circ - \Psi_r^* \tag{2.5}$$

which results in an optimal DOAP with a maximum absolute value of the determinant given by:

$$\det_{\max} := \max_{\mathbf{A}} |\det \mathbf{A}| = |\det \mathbf{A}_{\text{DOAP}}| = \sqrt{3}/144 \approx 0.012 \; .$$

The determinant of a DOAP without retarders is given by [AD03, Neg16]:

$$\frac{1}{4}R_u^2T_u^2(\cos 2\Psi_r - \cos 2\Psi_t)\sin 2\Psi_r \sin 2\Psi_t \sin(\Delta_r - \Delta_t)\,. \quad (2.6)$$

To measure how close a special design of the DOAP reaches the optimal value, the normalized determinant is defined as follows [AS05]:

$$|\det \mathbf{A}|_{\text{norm}} := \frac{|\det \mathbf{A}|}{\det_{\max}}\,. \quad (2.7)$$

Another, more common although less elegant way to assess the optimality of a DOAP is to calculate the condition number of the instrument matrix $\mathbf{A}$:

$$\text{cond}(\mathbf{A}) = \frac{\sigma_{\max}}{\sigma_{\min}}$$

where $\sigma_{\max}$ is the maximum and $\sigma_{\min}$ the minimum singular value resulting from a singular value decomposition. If $\sigma_1, \ldots, \sigma_n$ are the singular values of a non-singular instrument matrix $\mathbf{A}$, we obtain:

$$|\det \mathbf{A}| = \prod_i \sigma_i\,.$$

The optimal condition number has the following value:

$$\text{cond}_{\min} := \min_{\mathbf{A}} \text{cond}(\mathbf{A}) = \text{cond}(\mathbf{A}_{\text{DOAP}}) = \sqrt{3} \approx 1.732\,.$$

Analogous to Equation (2.7), we define the normalized condition number as:

$$\text{cond}_{\text{norm}}(\mathbf{A}) = \frac{\text{cond}_{\min}}{\text{cond}(\mathbf{A})}\,.$$

The normalized determinant $|\det \mathbf{A}|_{\text{norm}}$ and condition number $\text{cond}_{\text{norm}}(\mathbf{A})$ are the two quality measures we will use in this report to compare different designs of the DOAP and their influence on the sensitivity coefficients. For a DOAP without retarders the following holds by definition:

$$|\det \mathbf{A}_{\text{DOAP}}|_{\text{norm}} = \text{cond}_{\text{norm}}(\mathbf{A}_{\text{DOAP}}) = 1\,.$$

One major problem of the design of the DOAP without retarders is the realization of the beam splitter BS_i, which has to satisfy Equations (2.2), (2.3), (2.4) and (2.5) simultaneously. In fact, in Equation (1.12) it has been shown that Equation (2.5) follows directly from Equation (2.2). Therefore, a non-absorbing beam splitter BS_i only has to fulfill three constraints instead of four. However, the realization can still be complex as has been shown in [YSZL14] with a multilayer dielectric filter. Although that design has a normalized determinant of about 1, the DOAP is only applicable at a specific design wavelength and $|\det \mathbf{A}|_{\text{norm}}$ decreases quickly apart from that wavelength.

3 DOAP with Retarders

A further step to simplify BS_i has been proposed in our previous work [Neg16] and also by [ZCTH17]. A simple possibility to reduce the number of optimality constraints imposed on BS_i is to eliminate Equation (2.3). This can be achieved by positioning additional rotated retarders on the reflected and transmitted path. A design of the DOAP with rotated retarders is shown in Figure 1.1 where δ_r and δ_t are the retardances and β_r and β_t the rotational angles of the retarders on the reflected and transmitted light path, respectively. The instrument matrix of the DOAP without retarders is dependent on the optical parameters of BS_i:

$$\mathbf{A}_{\text{DOAP}} = \mathbf{A}_{\text{DOAP}}(R_u, T_u, \Psi_r, \Psi_t, \Delta_r, \Delta_t) \; .$$

We examine the influence of different designs of the DOAP on the normalized determinant and condition number. The influence of different designs of the DOAP is evaluated by using two different standard beam splitters $BS^{\dagger}$ and $BS^{\ddagger}$. The following desings of the DOAP are examined:

- DOAP without retarders
- DOAP with one variable retarder
- DOAP with two quarter-wave plates, one on each path
- DOAP with four quarter-wave plates, two on each path
- DOAP with two quarter-wave plates on the reflected path

In [ZCTH17] a beam splitter BS_i with the following optical parameters has been used:

$$\begin{aligned} R_u^\dagger &= 0.5, & T_u^\dagger &= 0.5, \\ \Psi_r^\dagger &= 21.04^\circ, & \Psi_t^\dagger &= 66.27^\circ, \\ \Delta_r^\dagger &= 188.19^\circ, & \Delta_t^\dagger &= 6.83^\circ \end{aligned}$$

which will be denoted as $BS^\dagger$. The beam splitter used in [Neg16] has the following optical parameters:

$$\begin{aligned} R_u^\ddagger &= 0.5, & T_u^\ddagger &= 0.5, \\ \Psi_r^\ddagger &= 20.65^\circ, & \Psi_t^\ddagger &= 69.74^\circ, \\ \Delta_r^\ddagger &= 150.06^\circ, & \Delta_t^\ddagger &= 0.16^\circ \end{aligned}$$

and will be denoted as $BS^\ddagger$. Using the DOAP without retarders, we get the following normalized determinant and condition number for the beam splitters $BS^\dagger$ and $BS^\ddagger$:

$$\begin{aligned} |\det \mathbf{A}_{\text{DOAP}}(R_u^\dagger, T_u^\dagger, \Psi_r^\dagger, \Psi_t^\dagger, \Delta_r^\dagger, \Delta_t^\dagger)|_{\text{norm}} &= 0.022, \\ |\det \mathbf{A}_{\text{DOAP}}(R_u^\ddagger, T_u^\ddagger, \Psi_r^\ddagger, \Psi_t^\ddagger, \Delta_r^\ddagger, \Delta_t^\ddagger)|_{\text{norm}} &= 0.42, \\ \text{cond}_{\text{norm}}(\mathbf{A}_{\text{DOAP}}(R_u^\dagger, T_u^\dagger, \Psi_r^\dagger, \Psi_t^\dagger, \Delta_r^\dagger, \Delta_t^\dagger)) &= 0.014, \\ \text{cond}_{\text{norm}}(\mathbf{A}_{\text{DOAP}}(R_u^\ddagger, T_u^\ddagger, \Psi_r^\ddagger, \Psi_t^\ddagger, \Delta_r^\ddagger, \Delta_t^\ddagger)) &= 0.29\,. \end{aligned}$$

For the DOAP without retarders it follows that $BS^\ddagger$ would be more suitable than $BS^\dagger$ because the latter would result into a nearly singular instrument matrix. The reason is obvious if we look at the determinant from Equation (2.6). The value of $\Delta_r^\dagger - \Delta_t^\dagger = 181.37^\circ$ for $BS^\dagger$ is nearly 180°, which results in a very low value of the normalized determinant and hence a nearly singular instrument matrix. The value of $\Delta_r^\ddagger - \Delta_t^\ddagger = 149.9^\circ$ is still bad compared to the optimum 90°, but the instrument matrix is not singular. As has been shown in [Neg16], the determinant of the instrument matrix $\mathbf{A}$ can be decomposed into two factors. The first factor is dependent on R_u, T_u, Ψ_r and Ψ_t and the second one on Δ_r and Δ_t and other retardances. This factorization is valid for all designs previously mentioned. For an arbitrary instrument matrix of a DOAP with retarders $\mathbf{A}$ we get the following proportionality:

$$\det \mathbf{A} \propto R^2 T^2 (\cos 2\Psi_r - \cos 2\Psi_t) \sin 2\Psi_r \sin 2\Psi_t\,. \tag{3.1}$$

The consequence of Equation (3.1) is that Ψ_r and Ψ_t impose a lower bound on the the sensitivity coefficients of a DOAP with retarders for any non-absorbing BS_i with $R = T = 0.5$, which is our main focus. If the values of $\Delta_r^\dagger - \Delta_t^\dagger$ and $\Delta_r^\ddagger - \Delta_t^\ddagger$ would be optimal i.e. $\Delta_r^\dagger - \Delta_t^\dagger = \Delta_r^\ddagger - \Delta_t^\ddagger = 90°$, we would get the following normalized determinants and condition numbers:

$$
\begin{aligned}
|\det \mathbf{A}_{\text{DOAP}}(R_u^\dagger, T_u^\dagger, \Psi_r^\dagger, \Psi_t^\dagger, 0, 90°)|_{\text{norm}} &= 0.91, \\
|\det \mathbf{A}_{\text{DOAP}}(R_u^\ddagger, T_u^\ddagger, \Psi_r^\ddagger, \Psi_t^\ddagger, 0, 90°)|_{\text{norm}} &= 0.84, \\
\text{cond}_{\text{norm}}(\mathbf{A}_{\text{DOAP}}(R_u^\dagger, T_u^\dagger, \Psi_r^\dagger, \Psi_t^\dagger, 0, 90°)) &= 0.82, \\
\text{cond}_{\text{norm}}(\mathbf{A}_{\text{DOAP}}(R_u^\ddagger, T_u^\ddagger, \Psi_r^\ddagger, \Psi_t^\ddagger, 0, 90°)) &= 0.80\,.
\end{aligned}
\tag{3.2}
$$

For the two beam splitters $BS^\dagger$ and $BS^\ddagger$ these are the optimal values that can be achieved with different designs of the DOAP with retarders. The retarders compensate suboptimal values of Δ_r and Δ_t, but cannot compensate suboptimal values of Ψ_r and Ψ_t. For the rest of the work we will therefore denote any design with retarders as optimal, if both quality measures are maximized for suboptimal values of Δ_r and Δ_t. As an example, the values of the quality measures for a specific design of the DOAP with the beam splitters $BS^\dagger$ and $BS^\ddagger$ must equal to those in Equation (3.2).

One very simple way to get an optimal DOAP with retarders is to mount a retarder e.g. on the reflected path with a variable retardance δ_r. We denote the instrument matrix as $\mathbf{A}_\delta$:

$$
\mathbf{A}_\delta(R_u, T_u, \Psi_r, \Psi_t, \Delta_r, \Delta_t, \delta_r) =
\begin{pmatrix}
\boldsymbol{q} \cdot \mathbf{M}_P(45°) & \cdot \mathbf{M}_\Delta(\delta_r, 0°) \cdot \mathbf{M}_S(\Psi_r, \Delta_r, R_u) \\
\boldsymbol{q} \cdot \mathbf{M}_P(-45°) & \cdot \mathbf{M}_\Delta(\delta_r, 0°) \cdot \mathbf{M}_S(\Psi_r, \Delta_r, R_u) \\
\boldsymbol{q} \cdot \mathbf{M}_P(45°) & \cdot \mathbf{M}_S(\Psi_t, \Delta_t, T_u) \\
\boldsymbol{q} \cdot \mathbf{M}_P(-45°) & \cdot \mathbf{M}_S(\Psi_t, \Delta_t, T_u)
\end{pmatrix} .
$$

Because the retardances on the reflected path accumulate, Equation (2.3) leads to the following condition to get an optimal DOAP:

$$
\delta_r + \Delta_r - \Delta_t = \pm 90° \Leftrightarrow \delta_r = \pm 90° - \Delta_r + \Delta_t
$$

and we denote the optimal values for $BS^\dagger$ and $BS^\ddagger$ as $\delta^\dagger$ and $\delta^\ddagger$, respectively.

If we choose the retardance in that way, we get an optimal DOAP and the same values for the normalized determinant and condition number as in Equation (3.2):

$$
\begin{aligned}
|\det \mathbf{A}_\delta(R_u^\dagger, T_u^\dagger, \Psi_r^\dagger, \Psi_t^\dagger, \Delta_r^\dagger, \Delta_t^\dagger, \delta_r^\dagger)|_{\text{norm}} &= 0.91,\\
|\det \mathbf{A}_\delta(R_u^\ddagger, T_u^\ddagger, \Psi_r^\ddagger, \Psi_t^\ddagger, \Delta_r^\ddagger, \Delta_t^\ddagger, \delta_r^\ddagger)|_{\text{norm}} &= 0.84,\\
\text{cond}_{\text{norm}}(\mathbf{A}_\delta(R_u^\dagger, T_u^\dagger, \Psi_r^\dagger, \Psi_t^\dagger, \Delta_r^\dagger, \Delta_t^\dagger, \delta_r^\dagger)) &= 0.82,\\
\text{cond}_{\text{norm}}(\mathbf{A}_\delta(R_u^\ddagger, T_u^\ddagger, \Psi_r^\ddagger, \Psi_t^\ddagger, \Delta_r^\ddagger, \Delta_t^\ddagger, \delta_r^\ddagger)) &= 0.80\ .
\end{aligned}
$$

Although we get optimal results, the problem with this design is that we need a special retarder. This has several disadvantages compared to retarders produced in bulk such as lower precision and higher cost. Quarter-wave plates are therefore of special interest. In [ZCTH17] a design has been proposed with two rotated quarter-wave plates, one on each path. Calculations revealed that they are better suited than half wave plates. In [Neg16] it has been figured out, that one quarter-wave plate on each path can improve the results, but does not produce optimal results for all values of Δ_r and Δ_t. Instead, a design with two quarter-wave plates on each path has been suggested which is optimal for all values of Δ_r and Δ_t.

First, we will examine the design of the DOAP with one quarter-wave plate on each path and let β_r and β_t be the rotational angles of the quarter-wave plates on the reflected and transmitted path, respectively. Let $\mathbf{A}_{Q_r,Q_t}$ be the corresponding instrument matrix:

$$
\mathbf{A}_{Q_r,Q_t}(R_u, T_u, \Psi_r, \Psi_t, \Delta_r, \Delta_t, \beta_r, \beta_t) =
\begin{pmatrix}
\boldsymbol{q}\cdot\mathbf{M}_P(45^\circ) & \cdot\mathbf{M}_Q(\beta_r) & \cdot\mathbf{M}_S(\Psi_r, \Delta_r, R_u)\\
\boldsymbol{q}\cdot\mathbf{M}_P(-45^\circ) & \cdot\mathbf{M}_Q(\beta_r) & \cdot\mathbf{M}_S(\Psi_r, \Delta_r, R_u)\\
\boldsymbol{q}\cdot\mathbf{M}_P(45^\circ) & \cdot\mathbf{M}_Q(\beta_t) & \cdot\mathbf{M}_S(\Psi_t, \Delta_t, T_u)\\
\boldsymbol{q}\cdot\mathbf{M}_P(-45^\circ) & \cdot\mathbf{M}_Q(\beta_t) & \cdot\mathbf{M}_S(\Psi_t, \Delta_t, T_u)
\end{pmatrix}.
$$

For the normalized determinant and condition number we get the following values:

$$
\begin{aligned}
|\det \mathbf{A}_{Q_r,Q_t}(R_u^\dagger, T_u^\dagger, \Psi_r^\dagger, \Psi_t^\dagger, \Delta_r^\dagger, \Delta_t^\dagger, \delta_r^\dagger)|_{\text{norm}} &= 0.91,\\
|\det \mathbf{A}_{Q_r,Q_t}(R_u^\ddagger, T_u^\ddagger, \Psi_r^\ddagger, \Psi_t^\ddagger, \Delta_r^\ddagger, \Delta_t^\ddagger, \delta_r^\ddagger)|_{\text{norm}} &= 0.79,\\
\text{cond}_{\text{norm}}(\mathbf{A}_{Q_r,Q_t}(R_u^\dagger, T_u^\dagger, \Psi_r^\dagger, \Psi_t^\dagger, \Delta_r^\dagger, \Delta_t^\dagger, \delta_r^\dagger)) &= 0.82,\\
\text{cond}_{\text{norm}}(\mathbf{A}_{Q_r,Q_t}(R_u^\ddagger, T_u^\ddagger, \Psi_r^\ddagger, \Psi_t^\ddagger, \Delta_r^\ddagger, \Delta_t^\ddagger, \delta_r^\ddagger)) &= 0.69\ .
\end{aligned}
\tag{3.3}
$$

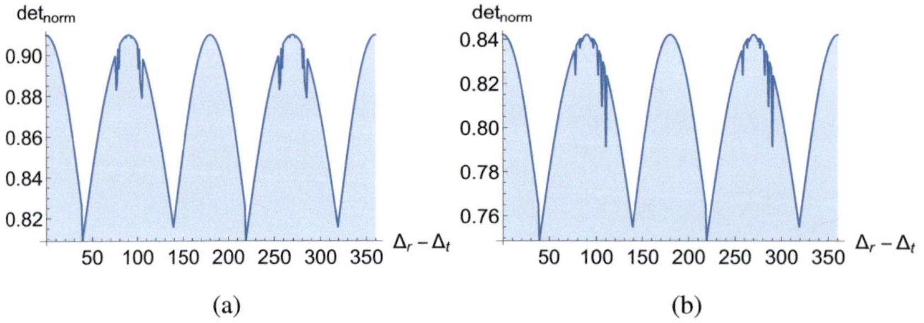

Figure 3.1: Normalized determinant for $\Psi_r^\dagger, \Psi_t^\dagger$ (a) and $\Psi_r^\ddagger, \Psi_t^\ddagger$ (b) when the value of $\Delta_r - \Delta_t$ varies. The design of the DOAP contains one quarter-wave plate on each light path.

Comparing Equation (3.2) with Equation (3.3) reveals that while the normalized determinant and condition number retain their optimal values for $BS^\dagger$, the values are lower for $BS^\ddagger$. The problem of this design is that the normalized determinant and condition number are only optimal for some values of Δ_r and Δ_t. If we plot the normalized determinant dependent on $\Delta_r - \Delta_t$ we get the Figure 3.1. For every value of $\Delta_r - \Delta_t$, the quarter-wave plates are rotated to maximize the normalized determinant. For computing the rotational angles a nonlinear numerical optimization has been performed using *Mathematica*. For some values of $\Delta_r - \Delta_t$ this algorithm only finds a local instead of the global minimum. The discontinuities in Figure 3.1 reveal where the nonlinear optimization returned a local optimum. A more rigorous optimization algorithm would always find the global optimum due to the low dimensional search space.

To overcome the problem that this design is not optimal for all values of Δ_r and Δ_t, it has been suggested in [Neg16] to use two quarter-wave plates on each path instead of one. Using four quarter-wave plates results into optimal values of the quality measures for any value of Δ_r and Δ_t. But there is even a simpler design with only two quarter-wave plates. Equation (2.3) suggests that only the retardation of one path has to be adjusted because only the difference $\Delta_r - \Delta_t$ matters. Because four quarter-wave plates can compensate any suboptimal value of $\Delta_r - \Delta_t$, it seems adequate to assume that two rotated quarter-wave plates on a single path (e.g. the reflected path) have the same effect on the normalized

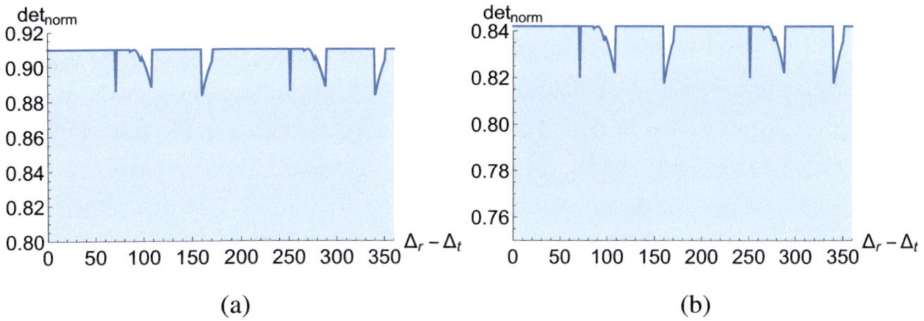

Figure 3.2: Normalized determinant for $\Psi_r^\dagger, \Psi_t^\dagger$ (a) and $\Psi_r^\ddagger, \Psi_t^\ddagger$ (b) when the value of $\Delta_r - \Delta_t$ varies. The design of the DOAP contains two quarter-wave plates on the reflected light path.

determinant as a variable retarder. The instrument matrix for two rotated quarter-wave plates on the reflected path is given by:

$$\mathbf{A}_{2Q_r}(R_u, T_u, \Psi_r, \Psi_t, \Delta_r, \Delta_t, \beta_r, \beta_r') =$$
$$\begin{pmatrix} \boldsymbol{q} \cdot \mathbf{M}_P(45^\circ) & \cdot\mathbf{M}_Q(\beta_r') \cdot \mathbf{M}_Q(\beta_r) \cdot \mathbf{M}_S(\Psi_r, \Delta_r, R_u) \\ \boldsymbol{q} \cdot \mathbf{M}_P(-45^\circ) & \cdot\mathbf{M}_Q(\beta_r') \cdot \mathbf{M}_Q(\beta_r) \cdot \mathbf{M}_S(\Psi_r, \Delta_r, R_u) \\ \boldsymbol{q} \cdot \mathbf{M}_P(45^\circ) & \cdot\mathbf{M}_S(\Psi_t, \Delta_t, T_u) \\ \boldsymbol{q} \cdot \mathbf{M}_P(-45^\circ) & \cdot\mathbf{M}_S(\Psi_t, \Delta_t, T_u) \end{pmatrix}$$

where β_r is the rotational angle of the first and β_r' of the second quarter-wave plate. Figure 3.2 shows the normalized determinant for any value of $\Delta_r - \Delta_t$. Ignoring the local optima of the nonlinear optimization, we see that we always get the same value for the normalized determinant which corresponds to the optimal value given in Equation (3.2).

4 Summary and Outlook

In this report a simple design of a DOAP has been proposed consisting of two quarter-wave plates on the reflected path. It has been shown that this design is better than mounting one quarter-wave plate on each path, because the negative effects on the sensitivity coefficients resulting from beam splitters with suboptimal retardances can always be compensated. Furthermore, calculations suggest that for any optimal DOAP analyzed in this report, the normalized determinant and condition number are optimal at the same rotational angles of the retarders. In future work this equivalence will be examined in more detail to better understand in which case we get the same results for both quality measures. Furthermore, analytical solutions for calculating the rotational angles for different designs will be provided. In future work it is also planned to provide other designs of practical relevance, especially designs which are applicable at a broad wavelength range.

Bibliography

[AD03] Azzam, R. M. A. and A. De. Optimal beam splitters for the division-of-amplitude photopolarimeter. *Journal of the Optical Society of America A*, 20(5):955, 2003.

[AS05] Azzam, R. M. A. and Faisal F. Sudradjat. Single-layer-coated beam splitters for the division-of-amplitude photopolarimeter. *Applied Optics*, 44(2):190, 2005.

[Azz82] R. M. A. Azzam. Division-of-amplitude Photopolarimeter (DOAP) for the Simultaneous Measurement of All Four Stokes Parameters of Light. *Optica Acta: International Journal of Optics*, 29(5):685–689, 1982.

[BPLF16] Jürgen Beyerer, Fernando Puente León, and Christian Frese. *Machine Vision : Automated Visual Inspection: Theory, Practice and Applications*. SpringerLink : Bücher. Springer, Berlin and Heidelberg, 1st ed. 2016 edition, 2016.

[DAP94b] Dupertuis, M. A., B. Acklin, and M. Proctor. Generalized energy balance and reciprocity relations for thin-film optics. *J. Opt. Soc. Am. A*, 11(3):1167–1174, Mar 1994.

[Fuj07] Hiroyuki Fujiwara. *Spectroscopic ellipsometry: Principles and applications*. John Wiley & Sons, Chichester and England and Hoboken and NJ, 2007.

[Hec02] Eugene Hecht. *Optics*. Addison-Wesley, Reading and Mass, 4th ed edition, 2002.

[HMS80] P. S. Hauge, R. H. Muller, and C. G. Smith. Conventions and formulas for using the Mueller-Stokes calculus in ellipsometry. *Surface Science*, 96(1-3):81–107, 1980.

[JCG08] JCGM. Evaluation of measurement data – Guide to the expression of uncertainty in measurement. Technical report, Joint Committee for Guides in Metrology (JCGM), 2008.

[Neg16] Christian Negara. Fast polarization state detection by division-of-amplitude in a simple configuration setup. In *Proceedings of the 2015 Joint Workshop of Fraunhofer IOSB and Institute for Anthropomatics, Vision and Fusion Laboratory*, Karlsruher Schriften zur Anthropomatik ; 24, pages 75–89, Karlsruhe, 2016. KIT Scientific Publishing.

[TM99] Harland G. Tompkins and William A. McGahan. *Spectroscopic ellipsometry and reflectometry: A user's guide*. Wiley, New York, 1999.

[YSZL14] Wenjia Yuan, Weidong Shen, Yueguang Zhang, and Xu Liu. Dielectric multilayer beam splitter with differential phase shift on transmission and reflection for division-of-amplitude photopolarimeter. *Optics Express*, 22(9):11011, 2014.

[ZCTH17] Liangwei Zeng, Yuanjing Cai, Chushen Tan, and Zuohua Huang. Optimization of stokes optical polarization measurement system. *Laser Technology*, 41(1):74, 2017.

Generating Object Proposals for Vehicle Detection in Aerial Images

Lars Sommer

Vision and Fusion Laboratory
Institute for Anthropomatics
Karlsruhe Institute of Technology (KIT), Germany
lars.sommer@kit.edu

Technical Report IES-2016-08

Abstract: Vehicle detection in aerial images is an important task in many applications such as screening of large areas or traffic monitoring. In general, classifiers or a cascade of classifiers within a sliding window approach are used to perform vehicle detection. However, sliding window approaches are limited for vehicle detection in a real-time system due to the huge number of windows to classify. To overcome this challenge, several objects proposals methods have been proposed for generating candidate windows in detection frameworks. Impressive results have been achieved on common detection benchmark datasets like Pascal VOC 2007 for a significantly reduced number of candidate windows. However, these datasets, which are used to develop the object proposals methods, exhibit considerably differing characteristics compared to aerial images. In this report, we examine the applicability of such object proposals methods for vehicle detection in aerial images. Therefore, we evaluate the performance of seven state-of-the-art object proposals methods on the publicly available DLR 3K Munich Vehicle Aerial Image Dataset. Relevant adaptions are highlighted by using the Selective Search method. Finally, the adapted methods are compared to baseline approaches like sliding window.

1 Introduction

Detecting vehicles is an important task in many applications such as screening of large areas or traffic monitoring. In general, vehicle detection in aerial images is performed by applying classifiers or a cascade of classifiers within a sliding window approach [LM15]. A search window of a certain scale is shifted horizontally and vertically across the entire image and appearance features are calculated at each window position. The calculated features are used as input for a classifier, which returns a confidence value for the occurrence of a vehicle. However, the huge number of candidate windows to classify limits the applicability in a real-time system, especially in case of different scales, aspect ratios, and orientations [HBDS16].

In literature, there exist several approaches to overcome this challenge in case of aerial images [CH16]. These approaches include reducing the search space or applying a cascade of weak classifiers. Reducing the search space is generally performed by incorporating road maps as provided from Geographic Information Systems (GIS) [LRK+14, TKRS13]. However, such approaches are limited to georeferenced images and areas occupied by road maps [LM15]. An alternative approach is to initially detect areas of interest, e.g. roads [MZM15]. However, in this case all relevant objects have to be present on roads. Otherwise, objects offside the road that might be of interest can be missed.

In the context of this report, we examine the applicability of object proposals methods for vehicle detection in aerial images. Object proposals methods generate a set of regions that are likely to contain an object [ADF12]. In recent years, several object proposals methods have been proposed to reduce the number of windows to classify. However, these methods are all explored on common detection benchmark datasets like Pascal VOC 2007 [EVGW+10] that significantly differ from aerial images. Typically, images of these datasets contain only one or few objects that are centered and occupy a high fraction of the entire image, whereas aerial images can contain multiple objects that are comparable small and randomly located. Though, there exist comprehensive surveys on state-of-the-art object proposals methods [HBDS16, CAMB15], there exists no literature about the applicability of these methods for considerably differing datasets as in case of aerial images.

In this report, we evaluate seven state-of-the-art object proposals methods on the publicly available DLR 3K Munich Vehicle Aerial Image Dataset [LM15]. This dataset consists of 20 images with a resolution of 5616×3744 pixels and a ground sampling distance of approximately 13 cm. Each image contains about 500 vehicles on average. To compensate for the differing characteristics of aerial images, we adapt each method. Therefore, we systematically analyze the impact of different parameters and extensions for each method separately. Relevant adaptions are highlighted exemplarily for the Selective Search method [UvdSGS13]. Finally, we compare the adapted methods to baseline approaches like sliding window to show how the number of candidate windows can be clearly reduced.

Method	Approach
GOP [KK14]	Grouping
LPO [KK15]	Grouping
Randomized Prim's [MGVG13]	Grouping
Selective Search [UvdSGS13]	Grouping
Edge Boxes [ZD14]	Window Scoring
Objectness [ADF12]	Window Scoring
Rahtu [RKB11]	Window Scoring

Table 2.1: Evaluated object proposals methods.

2 Object Proposals Methods

In literature, there exists a variety of different object proposals methods. These methods can be distinguished into *grouping methods* and *window scoring methods* [CAMB15, HBDS16]. *Grouping methods* are typically based on initial image segmentation followed by grouping segments. Therefore, a diverse set of cues such as appearance cues, color histogram, segment size, and boundary estimates are used. *Window scoring methods* are based on an initial set of candidate windows, for example, generated by a sliding window approach or random sampling. For each candidate window, multiple cues are used to calculate a score that is used to rank or filter candidate windows. An overview about the object proposals methods evaluated in the context of this report are given in Table 2.1. A more detailed description about these methods and their fundamental functionality is given in [HBDS16].

In the following, we give a short description of the fundamental functionality of the Selective Search method [UvdSGS13] that has been broadly used for generating candidate windows in detection frameworks like Fast R-CNN [Gir15]. Selective Search belongs to the *grouping methods*. Initially, a set of small starting segments is generated by the segmentation approach proposed by Felzenszwalb and Huttenlocher [FH04]. The size of these segments is adjustable by a threshold parameter k. Larger values for k result in larger segments. In the next step, similarities between all neighbouring segments are calculated and the most similar segments are merged together until a single segment covers the entire image. All segments are considered as object proposals except for segments whose dimensions fall below a previously set minimal height or width. Four complementary similarity measures as well as combinations of the different measures are used to measure the similarity between neighbouring regions. The used similarity measures are s_{colour}, $s_{texture}$, s_{size}, and s_{fill}. A detailed description of these measures is given in [UvdSGS13]. To generate a set of highly diverse object proposals, different colour spaces and varying threshold parameter k are used to generate differing segments and different similarity measures or combinations are applied. Typically, 80 different combinations of segmentation settings and similarity measures are used in total.

3 Experimental Results

In this section, we evaluate the performance of seven object proposals methods on the publicly available DLR 3K Munich Vehicle Aerial Image Dataset. The used dataset consists of 20 images with a resolution of 5616×3744 pixels. For our experiments, each image is divided into tiles of 936×624 pixels. Image sections are exemplarily shown in Figure 3.1. First, we provide results of the original object proposals methods. Then, we show the impact of relevant adaptions by means of Selective Search. Finally, we present the results of the adapted approaches. The source code of all selected methods is publicly available.

To evaluate the performance, we apply metrics that are functions of intersection over union (IoU). IoU is calculated by

$$IoU = \frac{A_{proposal} \cap A_{GT}}{A_{proposal} \cup A_{GT}},$$

where $A_{proposal}$ and A_{GT} are the area of the proposals and the ground truth bounding boxes, respectively. Values close to 1 indicate a high similarity, whereas values close to 0 indicate a low similarity between proposed bounding boxes and GT bounding boxes. Typically, an IoU value of 0.5 is used to accept GT objects as recalled in detection tasks [EVGW+10]. Recall-IoU curves are used to examine the detection rate of each method. Therefore, we vary the minimal IoU used as threshold value to consider GT boxes as recalled or not. We further plot the recall with respect to the number of proposals for a fixed IoU threshold to examine the impact of the number of proposals.

Figure 3.1: Image sections of the DLR 3K Munich Vehicle Aerial Image Dataset [LM15]

3.1 Original Object Proposals Methods

At first, we evaluate the performance of the original object proposals methods. Therefore, we apply the original algorithms and parameters as proposed in the corresponding literature. Figure 3.2 shows the corresponding recall-IoU curves. For IoU threshold values below 0.2, several approaches exhibit recall values close to 1. However, the recall values decrease considerably with increasing threshold values. The Selective Search method that outperforms all other methods exhibits a recall value less than 0.9 for an IoU threshold of 0.5 so that more than 10% of all GT objects are not considered as recalled. The recall values achieved for the other methods are even worse. Hence, the original algorithms and parameters are not well suited for generating candidate windows in aerial images.

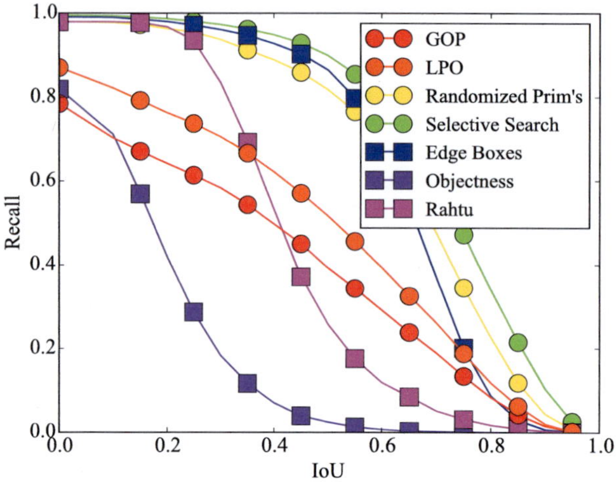

Figure 3.2: Recall-IoU curves of the original object proposals methods

3.2 Adaptation to Aerial Images

Reason for the high number of missed GT objects is that all methods are developed for generating proposals in significantly differing datasets. Thus, we systematically analyzed the impact of different parameters and adapted each method separately. In the following, the performed adaptions are exemplarily discussed for the Selective Search method.

A substantial difference between the characteristics of the detection benchmark datasets and aerial images is the size of the occurring objects. As in the detection benchmark datasets object dimensions are mostly in the range between 50 and 200 pixels, object proposals that height or width are less than 20 pixels are removed. However, aerial images can contain objects that are significantly smaller, so that smaller object proposals are required to account for small objects. Therefore, we reduce the minimal height and width to 5 pixels. As shown in Figure 3.3, the performance is considerably improved. Furthermore, the size of the object proposals is affected by the applied segmentation as smaller initial segments can result in smaller object proposals. Therefore, we vary the threshold

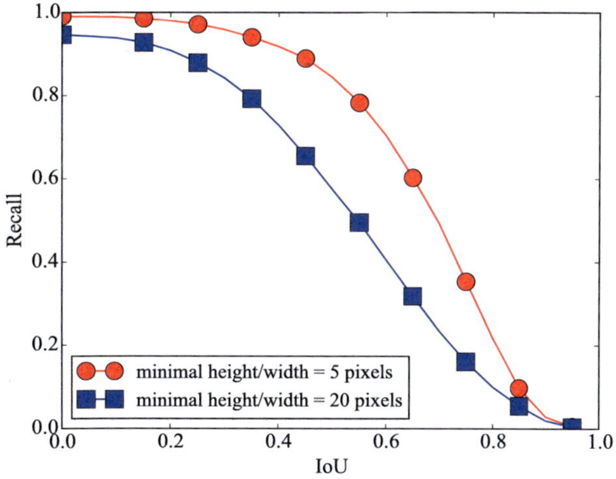

Figure 3.3: Recall-IoU curves for various minimal dimensions of the object proposals. Reducing the minimal dimensions to 5 pixels results in considerably improved recall values.

parameter k to generate initial segments with varying sizes. The corresponding recall-IoU curves are given in Figure 3.4. For IoU threshold values below 0.6, the recall values are increasing with smaller k due to smaller initial segments.

However, both adaptions result in an increased number of proposals. In case of applying 80 different combinations of segmentation settings and similarity measures, more than 300,000 object proposals are generated. To reduce the number of proposals, we analyze the impact of both different segmentation settings and different similarity measures. Figure 3.5 shows exemplarily the impact of applying different similarity measures. For IoU threshold values below 0.6, the best recall values are achieved for s_{size} that compares the size of neighbouring regions and encourages small regions to merge early so that regions are of similar sizes throughout the algorithm. The worst recall values are achieved by applying similarity measures combined with $s_{texture}$.

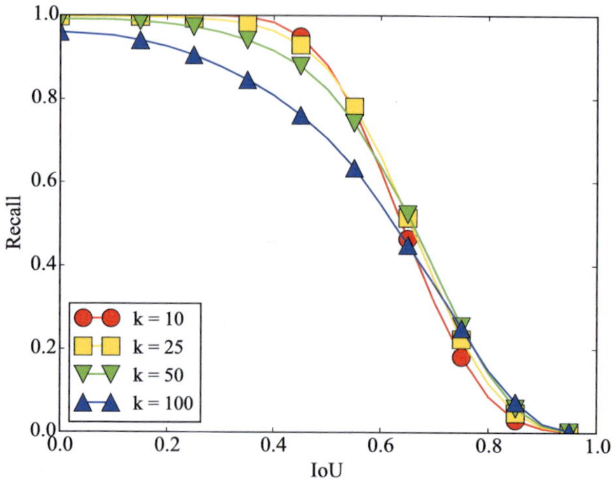

Figure 3.4: Recall-IoU curves for various segmentation threshold parameters k. Smaller values for k and consequently smaller initial regions result in better recall values for IoU threshold values below 0.6

The recall-IoU curves vary for different similarity measures as different sets of proposals are generated. To clarify how many sets of proposals have to be combined to achieve adequate recall values, we add steadily proposals generated for different similarity measures. As shown in Figure 3.6, the recall values are increasing with the number of combined proposals sets. However, the improvement becomes less with the number of proposals sets so that combining more than four proposals sets only results in negligible improvements. Similar results are observed for combing proposals sets generated for various colour spaces and for various segmentation threshold parameters k.

Originally, the generated object proposals are randomly sorted, as objects can have any scale. However, aerial images contain objects with certain scales. Therefore, we replace the random order with a weighted order based on the proposal size. As depicted in Figure 3.7, the weighted order clearly outperforms the random order since considerably less proposals are required to achieve comparable recall values.

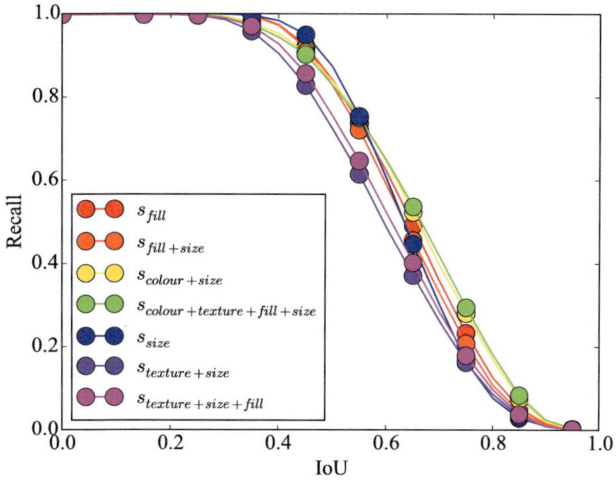

Figure 3.5: Recall-IoU curves for various similarity measures used to group segments. Applying s_{size} achieves the best recall values for IoU thresholds below 0.6.

3.3 Adapted Object Proposals Methods

Adaptations are performed for each method separately similar to Section 3.2. The corresponding recall-IoU curves are depicted in Figure 3.8. All methods show clearly improved recall values compared to the original methods. In case of *grouping methods*, adapting the size of initial segments exhibits the highest impact on the performance as shown for Selective Search in Section 3.2. The performance of *window scoring methods* is mainly improved by adapting the minimal and maximal dimensions of candidate windows to the object sizes. For IoU threshold values below 0.55, the method proposed by Rahtu et al. [RKB11] exhibts the best recall values and slightly outperforms Selective Search and Randomized Prim's. All adapted methods except LPO achieve recall values close to 1 for small IoU threshold values. We expect that the applied segmentation models, which are used for generating foreground and background masks are the reason for the low recall values, as these segmentation models are pre-trained on a dataset that considerably differs from aerial images.

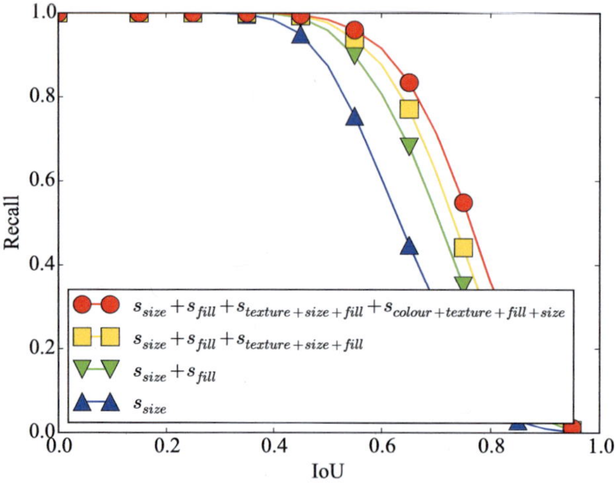

Figure 3.6: Recall-IoU curves for various combinations of proposals sets. The recall values are increasing with the number of proposals sets, though combing more than four sets of proposals only results in negligible improvements.

3.4 Comparison to Baseline Approaches

Finally, we compare the adapted methods to baseline approaches. Therefore, we consider a sliding window approach with three different window scales and random sampling of candidate windows. The dimensions of the randomly sampled candidate windows are in the range between 5 and 50 pixels. Figure 3.9 and 3.10 show exemplarily the comparison of the adapted Selective Search method, the original Selective Search method and both baseline approaches. The adapted Selective Search method exhibits better recall values for all IoU thresholds especially for IoU thresholds above 0.4. The recall value of the applied sliding window approach converges to 0.94 with increasing number of candidate windows for an IoU threshold of 0.5. Hence, the considered window scales are not enough. Even more scales and aspect ratios and consequently more candidate windows are necessary to achieve recall values close to 1.

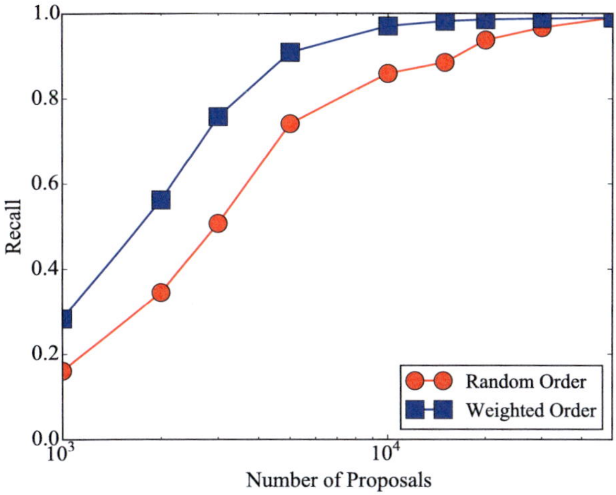

Figure 3.7: Recall as a function of the number of proposals for different order strategies. The random order is clearly outperformed by the weighted order based on the proposals size.

4 Conclusion

In the context of this report, we evaluated the applicability of seven object proposals methods for aerial images. We adapted each method separately to account for the characteristics of the aerial images that considerably differ from datasets used to explore these methods. Therefore, we systematically analyzed each method as exemplarily shown for Selective Search. In case of *grouping methods*, adapting the size of initial segments exhibited the highest impact on the performance, whereas the performance of *window scoring methods* is mainly improved by adapting the minimal and maximal dimensions of candidate windows to the object sizes. All adapted methods except LPO are suitable for aerial images as these methods achieve recall values close to 1. Finally, we demonstrated exemplarily for Selective Search that the number of candidate windows can be reduced compared to baseline approaches.

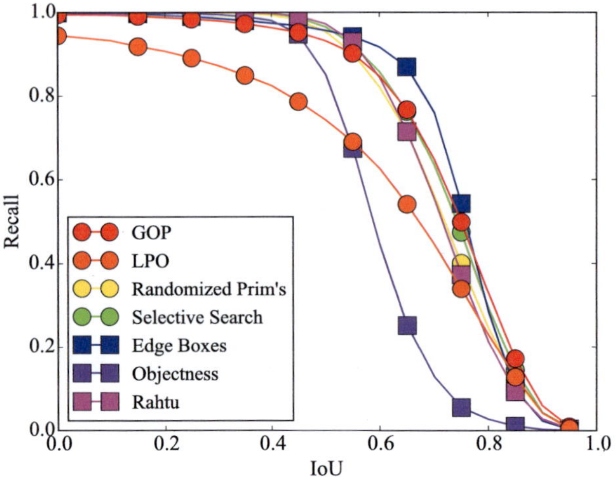

Figure 3.8: Recall-IoU curves of the adapted object proposals methods. All methods show clearly improved recall values compared to the original methods.

Bibliography

[ADF12] Bogdan Alexe, Thomas Deselaers, and Vittorio Ferrari. Measuring the objectness of image windows. *IEEE Transactions on Pattern Analysis and Machine Intelligence*, 34(11):2189–2202, 2012.

[CAMB15] Neelima Chavali, Harsh Agrawal, Aroma Mahendru, and Dhruv Batra. Object-proposal evaluation protocol is' gameable'. *arXiv preprint arXiv:1505.05836*, 2015.

[CH16] Gong Cheng and Junwei Han. A survey on object detection in optical remote sensing images. *ISPRS Journal of Photogrammetry and Remote Sensing*, 117:11–28, 2016.

[EVGW$^+$10] Mark Everingham, Luc Van Gool, Christopher KI Williams, John Winn, and Andrew Zisserman. The pascal visual object classes (voc) challenge. *International journal of computer vision*, 88(2):303–338, 2010.

[FH04] Pedro F Felzenszwalb and Daniel P Huttenlocher. Efficient graph-based image segmentation. *International Journal of Computer Vision*, 59(2):167–181, 2004.

[Gir15] Ross Girshick. Fast r-cnn. In *Proceedings of the IEEE International Conference on Computer Vision*, pages 1440–1448, 2015.

[HBDS16] Jan Hosang, Rodrigo Benenson, Piotr Dollár, and Bernt Schiele. What makes for effective detection proposals? *IEEE transactions on pattern analysis and machine intelligence*, 38(4):814–830, 2016.

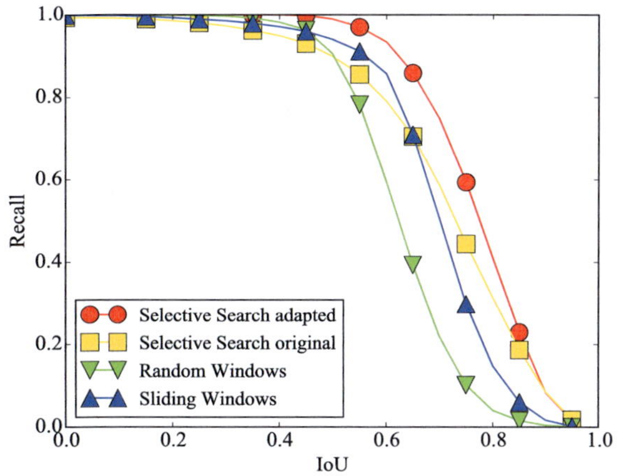

Figure 3.9: Recall-IoU curves of the adapted Selective Search method, the original Selective Search method and two baseline approaches. The adapted Selective Search method clearly outperforms all other methods.

[KK14] Philipp Krähenbühl and Vladlen Koltun. Geodesic object proposals. In *European Conference on Computer Vision*, pages 725–739. Springer, 2014.

[KK15] Philipp Krähenbühl and Vladlen Koltun. Learning to propose objects. In *2015 IEEE Conference on Computer Vision and Pattern Recognition (CVPR)*, pages 1574–1582. IEEE, 2015.

[LM15] K. Liu and G. Mattyus. Fast multiclass vehicle detection on aerial images. *Geoscience and Remote Sensing Letters, IEEE*, PP(99):1–5, 2015.

[LRK+14] Jens Leitloff, Dominik Rosenbaum, Franz Kurz, Oliver Meynberg, and Peter Reinartz. An operational system for estimating road traffic information from aerial images. *Remote Sensing*, 6(11):11315–11341, 2014.

[MGVG13] Santiago Manen, Matthieu Guillaumin, and Luc Van Gool. Prime object proposals with randomized prim's algorithm. In *Proceedings of the IEEE International Conference on Computer Vision*, pages 2536–2543, 2013.

[MZM15] Thomas Moranduzzo, Abdallah Zeggada, and Farid Melgani. A fast screening method for detecting cars in uav images over urban areas. In *2015 Joint Urban Remote Sensing Event (JURSE)*, pages 1–4. IEEE, 2015.

[RKB11] Esa Rahtu, Juho Kannala, and Matthew Blaschko. Learning a category independent object detection cascade. In *2011 International Conference on Computer Vision*, pages 1052–1059. IEEE, 2011.

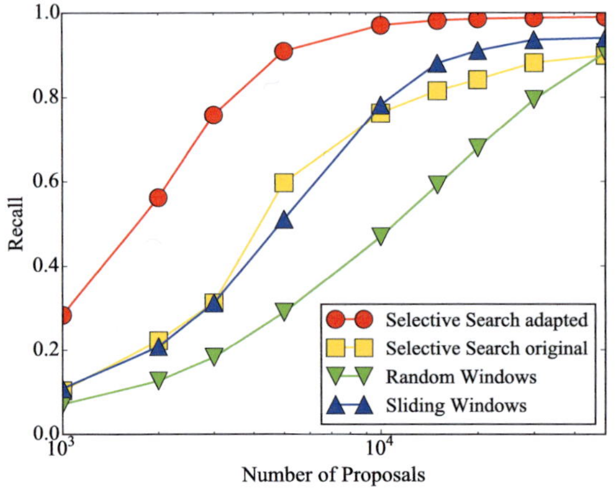

Figure 3.10: Recall as a funtion of the number of proposals for the adapted and original Selective Search method and two baseline approaches. The adapted Selective Search method clearly outperforms all other methods.

[TKRS13] Sebastian Tuermer, Franz Kurz, Peter Reinartz, and Uwe Stilla. Airborne vehicle detection in dense urban areas using hog features and disparity maps. *IEEE Journal of Selected Topics in Applied Earth Observations and Remote Sensing*, 6(6):2327–2337, 2013.

[UvdSGS13] Jasper RR Uijlings, Koen EA van de Sande, Theo Gevers, and Arnold WM Smeulders. Selective search for object recognition. *International journal of computer vision*, 104(2):154–171, 2013.

[Wen10] Jakob Wenzel. Mitsuba renderer, 2010. http://www.mitsuba-renderer.org.

[ZD14] C Lawrence Zitnick and Piotr Dollár. Edge boxes: Locating object proposals from edges. In *European Conference on Computer Vision*, pages 391–405. Springer, 2014.

Scale-related evolution of BRDFs

Alexey Pak

Vision and Fusion Laboratory
Institute for Anthropomatics
Karlsruhe Institute of Technology (KIT), Germany
alexey.pak@kit.edu

Technical Report IES-2016-09

Abstract: In computer graphics, objects are often modeled as polygonal meshes with flat facets, the reflection of light from facets is described by the so-called bi-directional reflectance distribution function (BRDF). Along with the intrinsic optical properties of the material, it captures the effects due to surface microstructure, i.e. shape features smaller than the facet size (and therefore not representable by the mesh model). If the typical facet size changes, some structures may switch from the "responsibility domain" of BRDFs to that of the geometric model, or vice versa. Therefore, for sufficiently complex surfaces, BRDFs are inherently scale-dependent. If one measures a BRDF at one scale, and applies at another, it must be adjusted ("evolved") according to the specific surface structure. In this report, we derive explicit BRDF evolution equations and discuss their implications.

1 Introduction

The geometrical complexity of a model that describes an arbitrary surface (for example, a desk) in general depends on the resolution of the chosen observation method. If we sample surface points at a distance of a few centimeters from each other, the resulting model will be rather smooth (e.g., the desk will appear almost flat). If the distance between the samples is of the order of micrometers, the model becomes extremely complex, with overlapping peaks and valleys. At even smaller scales, the object is no longer a surface but a collection of bound and free particles performing some complicated motions.

If we study the reflection of light from the model towards some detector (e.g., a camera pixel), we may usually limit ourselves with the geometrical optics (i.e. with scales much greater than the wavelength of light). To every scene and every camera setup, we may also associate some effective observation scale μ. It is typically determined by the resolution of the surface model as desribed above or by the size of the features resolved by the camera (whichever is greater). An efficient practical approach to capture the response of such a scene is to represent the "coarse" geometry (features of size larger than μ) by the mesh (re-deriving it from the original model, if necessary), and incapsulate the microscopic appearance into bi-directional reflectance distribution functions (BRDFs) [Bas01], associated with the flat facets of the mesh. BRDFs, therefore, provide an efficient way to characterize materials: they may be derived or measured once and used to render images of multiple objects under various conditions.

If the observation scale μ were fixed for all scenes and observation conditions, one could create a universal library of BRDFs for various materials (as is typically done in the development of video games). However, in reality the effective observation scale μ depends on the scene and the camera setup. At the same time, the surface may have features at some "characteristic" scale μ_c that significantly contribute to its optical appearance (consider, e.g., "orange-skin finish", "roughness", or "polishing artefacts"). Depending on whether μ is greater or smaller than μ_c, the BRDFs must significantly differ. One solution to this problem is to measure BRDFs at multiple scales and interpolate between them [TLQ$^+$02]. One needs then a massive database of measurements. An alternative is to derive the rules that govern the μ-related "evolution" of BRDFs, and generate them based on the measurements defined at some scale μ_0.

In this report, we formalize the notion of the scale-dependent evolution of BRDFs and suggest a simple integral equation connecting them with the surface statistics. For the simple case of isotropic (invariant with respect to rotations about the surface normal vector) BRDFs on nearly-planar surfaces, we manage to integrate the BRDF evolution equation in closed form. For the more general case of anisotropic surfaces, we demonstrate that upon a Fourier transform over the group of rotations, the equation factorizes and can be efficiently integrated numerically up to any finite frequency. Finally, we discuss the new exotic contributions in BRDFs ("plus-distributions") that may arise e.g. due to the scale evolution over some specially micro-structured surfaces.

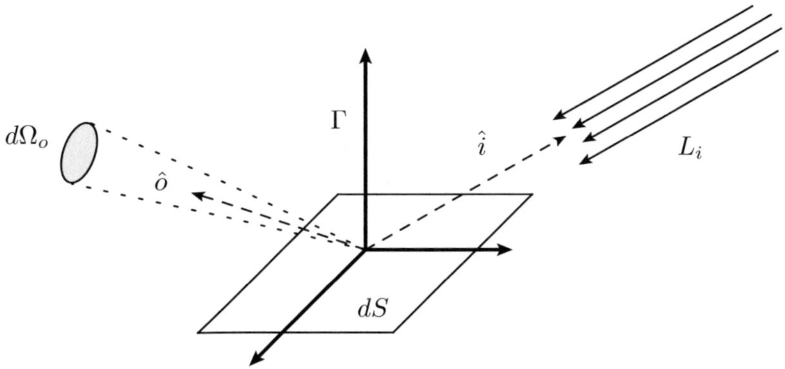

Figure 2.1: Reflection of light from a small surface element.

2 Notations

Let us consider a small surface element ϵ of area dS with some 3D orientation Γ, illuminated with a parallel beam of light coming from the direction $\hat{\imath}$. The incident intensity of the illumination (radiation power per cross-section area, watts per square meter) is L_i (Fig. 2.1). Our goal is to measure the directional distribution of the reflected and scattered light. To that end, we place a detector very far away from ϵ so that the direction towards the detector is $\hat{o}$ and its angular size as seen from ϵ is $d\Omega_o$. The BRDF $\beta(\hat{\imath}, \hat{o}, \Gamma)$ describes then the intensity I_o of light (power per unit of solid angle, watts per steradian) received by the detector:

$$I_o = L_i \; \beta(\hat{\imath}, \hat{o}, \Gamma) \; \left(\hat{\imath}^T \cdot \hat{n}(\Gamma)\right) \; d\Omega \; dS. \tag{2.1}$$

The geometrical factor $(\hat{\imath}^T \cdot \hat{n}(\Gamma))$ equals the cosine of angle between the incoming light direction $\hat{\imath}$ and the surface normal vector $\hat{n}(\Gamma)$ and accounts for the trivial change in the surface irradiation density as the surface incline changes. For convenience, in what follows we absorb his factor into the definition of BRDFs and define a function ρ as follows: $\rho(\hat{\imath}, \hat{o}, \Gamma) \equiv \beta(\hat{\imath}, \hat{o}, \Gamma) \; \left(\hat{\imath}^T \cdot \hat{n}(\Gamma)\right)$.

In a more detailed picture, ρ may further depend on the light wavelength λ, the incoming and the reflected light polarizations, coherence length, etc. We will focus here only on the dependence of ρ on the scale μ that separates "shape" from the "material properties", i.e. our primary object of interest will be the function $\rho(\hat{\imath}, \hat{o}, \Gamma, \mu)$.

The precise nature of the orientation Γ will be elaborated later. Here we only note that for isotropic surfaces and BRDFs, the actual orientation parameter is not Γ but the normal surface vector $\hat{n}(\Gamma)$. In particular, if the surface is an ideal flat mirror, its BRDF is

$$\rho_{\text{mirror}}(\hat{\imath}, \hat{o}, \hat{n}) = A\delta\left(\hat{n} - \hat{n}_s(\hat{\imath}, \hat{o})\right), \quad \text{where } \hat{n}_s(\hat{\imath}, \hat{o}) = \frac{\hat{\imath} + \hat{o}}{\|\hat{\imath} + \hat{o}\|},$$

and A is some normalization constant.

3 General BRDF consistency equation

Let us now choose some macroscopic surface patch E, illuminated with a parallel beam of light of uniform intensity L_i coming from the direction $\hat{\imath}$, and observe it with an infinitely distant detector along the direction $\hat{o}$. There are two alternative ways to describe the observed light intensity in the detector.

In the first case, we follow the picture above and consider the entire patch E as a single element with its global orientation Γ_∞ and the respective BRDF $\rho(\hat{\imath}, \hat{o}, \Gamma, \infty)$. The Eq. (2.1) then applies without modifications.

In the second case, we split E into many pieces of typical size μ, each reflecting the light according to Eq. (2.1) with the respective microscopic BRDF $\rho(\hat{\imath}, \hat{o}, \Gamma, \mu)$. The resulting detector response I_o will then be a sum of contributions from all the elements, each having its specific orientation.

If we knew the complete micro-geometry of the surface, we could directly compute this sum. More often, however, we deal with unknown geometries but know the specific nature of the surface, such as wood, leather, polished metal, etc. The geometry in this case may be characterized statistically in terms of some function $p(\Gamma_\infty, \Gamma, \mu)$ that denotes the probability to find an element with orientation Γ in the surface E given its global orientation Γ_∞. In particular, p must be consistent with the definition of the global orientation: $p(\Gamma_\infty, \Gamma, \mu) \overset{\mu\to\infty}{\to} \delta(\Gamma - \Gamma_\infty)$.

Regardless of our representation of the surface, the amount of light collected by the detector should not change, which leads us to the following condition[1]:

$$\rho(\hat{\imath}, \hat{o}, \Gamma_\infty, \infty) = \int \rho(\hat{\imath}, \hat{o}, \Gamma, \mu)\, p(\Gamma_\infty, \Gamma, \mu)\, d\Gamma. \tag{3.1}$$

The left hand side of Eq. (3.1) is independent of the scale μ. We therefore arrive at the basic consistency equation for BRDFs:

$$\partial_\mu \int \rho(\hat{\imath}, \hat{o}, \Gamma, \mu)\, p(\Gamma_\infty, \Gamma, \mu)\, d\Gamma = 0, \tag{3.2}$$

where we define $\partial_\mu \equiv \partial/\partial\mu$ and the integration runs over all distinct orientations in the 3D space.

4 Evolution for isotropic surfaces

As noted above, isotropic BRDFs and the statistics of isotropic surfaces depend only on the direction of the surface normal vector $\hat{n}$ and not on the rotation about $\hat{n}$. The re-formulated consistency condition in this case is

$$\partial_\mu \int \rho(\hat{\imath}, \hat{o}, \hat{n}, \mu)\, p(\hat{n}_\infty, \hat{n}, \mu)\, d\hat{n} = 0. \tag{4.1}$$

In order to decouple the evolution of the BRDF from that of the surface statistics, let us in addition assume that the surface only slightly deviates from a plane at all scales. This approximation can be formalized as follows. Let us choose the global vertical direction $\hat{z}$ and re-define ρ and p in terms of vectors $\vec{m}$ replacing the respective normal vectors $\hat{n}$:

$$\vec{m} = (\hat{n}^T \hat{z})^{-1} \hat{n} - \hat{z}.$$

In other words, $m_z \equiv 0$ and $(\vec{m} + \hat{z})$ is collinear with $\hat{n}$. Instead of $\hat{n}_\infty$, we now use $\vec{m}_\infty$, and instead of $\hat{n}$, we use $\vec{m}$, so that Eq. (4.1) becomes

$$\partial_\mu \int \rho(\hat{\imath}, \hat{o}, \vec{m}, \mu)\, p(\vec{m}_\infty, \vec{m}, \mu)\, dm_x dm_y = 0,$$

[1] This description can be compared to the microfacet BRDF model without the masking and shading effects, where some generic microscopic BRDF $\rho(\hat{\imath}, \hat{o}, \Gamma, \mu)$ is used instead of the Fresnel reflectance. As such, it applies only to non-grazing angles for $\hat{\imath}$ and $\hat{o}$, and nearly-flat surfaces: if an element has an incline that differs strongly from that of the global surface, the relevant probabilities will be dependent on the directions $\hat{\imath}$ and $\hat{o}$ via geometric factors.

where the integration runs over the entire two-dimensional plane.

The condition that a surface is almost flat means that all relevant normal vectors are only slightly deviating from the z-direction, i.e. $\|\vec{m}_\infty\| \ll 1$ and $p(\vec{m}_\infty, \vec{m}, \mu) = 0$ for all $\|\vec{m}\| > m_{max}$ with some $m_{max} \ll 1$. In this case, the two-dimensional distribution of the normal vectors as a function of $\vec{m}$ will have a peak centered at the point $\vec{m}_\infty$ and in the first approximation will preserve its shape as $\vec{m}_\infty$ varies:

$$p(\vec{m}_\infty, \vec{m}, \mu) = q(\vec{m}_\infty - \vec{m}, \mu).$$

The consistency equation now takes the form of a convolution:

$$\partial_\mu \int \rho(\hat{\imath}, \hat{o}, \vec{m}, \mu)\, q(\vec{m}_\infty - \vec{m}, \mu)\, d\vec{m} = \partial_\mu \left((\rho \star q)(\vec{m}_\infty)\right) = 0. \quad (4.2)$$

If we denote the 2D Fourier images of the functions $\rho(\hat{\imath}, \hat{o}, \vec{m}, \mu)$ and $q(\vec{m}, \mu)$ with respect to $\vec{m}$ as $R(\hat{\imath}, \hat{o}, \vec{W}, \mu)$, and $Q(\vec{W}, \mu)$, respectively, then Eq. (4.2) is equivalent to

$$\begin{aligned} &\partial_\mu \left(R(\hat{\imath}, \hat{o}, \vec{W}, \mu) Q(\vec{W}, \mu)\right) = 0, \quad \text{or} \\ &\partial_\mu \log R(\hat{\imath}, \hat{o}, \vec{W}, \mu) = -\partial_\mu \log Q(\vec{W}, \mu). \end{aligned} \quad (4.3)$$

(A trivial technical requirement here is that neither R nor Q may vanish inside the relevant domain of $\vec{W}$).

The solution of the Eq. (4.3) is trivial:

$$R(\hat{\imath}, \hat{o}, \vec{W}, \mu) = R(\hat{\imath}, \hat{o}, \vec{W}, \mu_0) \frac{Q(\vec{W}, \mu_0)}{Q(\vec{W}, \mu)}, \quad (4.4)$$

where μ_0 is some scale at which the BRDF is known. Using Eq. (4.4) and the actual statistics of the surface, one may easily produce BRDFs at any scale μ.

5 Evolution for anisotropic BRDFs and surfaces

In order to solve Eq. (3.2) in a more general case, we need to choose some explicit parameterization of orientations Γ in a three-dimensional space (in other words, choose some representation of the Lie group $SO(3)$ of 3D rotations). The most well-known representation of $SO(3)$ is the set of orthogonal 3×3 matrices with determinant $+1$. According to Euler, any 3D rotation may be represented as a function of three angles α, β, and γ such that $0 \leq \alpha, \gamma < 2\pi$, $0 \leq \beta < \pi$:

$$\Gamma(\alpha, \beta, \gamma) = U(\alpha) \cdot A(\beta) \cdot U(\gamma) \tag{5.1}$$

with

$$U(\alpha) = \begin{pmatrix} \cos\alpha & -\sin\alpha & 0 \\ \sin\alpha & \cos\alpha & 0 \\ 0 & 0 & 1 \end{pmatrix} \text{ and } A(\beta) = \begin{pmatrix} \cos\beta & 0 & \sin\beta \\ 0 & 1 & 0 \\ -\sin\beta & 0 & \cos\beta \end{pmatrix}. \tag{5.2}$$

Now let us consider the distribution $p(\Gamma_\infty, \Gamma, \mu)$. It is clear that a simultaneous rotation of the global orientation Γ_∞ and the element orientation Γ by some rotation matrix $\Delta \in SO(3)$ is equivalent to a global rotation of space, and the fraction of elements oriented at $\Delta \cdot \Gamma$ relative to $\Delta \cdot \Gamma_\infty$ remains invariant. We therefore have:

$$p(\Delta \cdot \Gamma_\infty, \Delta \cdot \Gamma, \mu) = p(\Gamma_\infty, \Gamma, \mu), \quad \text{or, equivalently,}$$
$$p(\Gamma_\infty, \Gamma, \mu) = q(\Gamma^{-1} \cdot \Gamma_\infty, \mu) \text{ for some function } q.$$

The respective evolution equation

$$\partial_\mu \int \rho(\hat{\imath}, \hat{o}, \Gamma, \mu)\, q(\Gamma^{-1} \cdot \Gamma_\infty, \mu)\, d\Gamma = \partial_\mu \left((\rho \star q)(\Gamma_\infty) \right) = 0 \tag{5.3}$$

now contains the canonical convolution over the group $SO(3)$. In order to transform this convolution into a product, we need to briefly recall the properties of the Fourier transform over the group of rotations (for more details, see [KR08]).

Any function $f(\alpha, \beta, \gamma)$ of the three angles α, β, and γ defined in Eqs. (5.1) and (5.2) can be represented as an infinite sum:

$$f(\alpha, \beta, \gamma) = \sum_{J=0}^{\infty} \sum_{M=-J}^{J} \sum_{M'=-J}^{J} f^J_{MM'}\, D^J_{MM'}(\alpha, \beta, \gamma), \quad \text{where}$$
$$f^J_{MM'} = \langle f, D^J_{MM'} \rangle = \frac{2J+1}{8\pi^2} \times$$
$$\times \int_0^{2\pi} d\alpha \int_0^{\pi} \sin\beta\, d\beta \int_0^{2\pi} d\gamma\, f(\alpha, \beta, \gamma)\, \left(D^J_{MM'}(\alpha, \beta, \gamma) \right)^*.$$

The basis functions here are the so-called Wigner D-functions:

$$D^J_{MM'}(\alpha, \beta, \gamma) = e^{-iM\alpha}\, e^{-iM'\gamma}\, d^J_{MM'}(\cos\beta),$$

and

$$\begin{aligned} d^J_{MM'}(t) = (-1)^{J-M'}\, 2^{-J} & \sqrt{\frac{(J+M)!}{(J+M')!(J-M')!(J-M)!}} \\ & \times (1-t)^{-(M-M')/2}(1+t)^{-(M+M')/2} \\ & \times \frac{d^{J-M}}{dt^{J-M}}\left[(1-t)^{J-M'}(1+t)^{J+M'}\right]. \end{aligned}$$

The Fourier transform of a convolution may be found as follows. If $f(\Gamma) \mapsto f^J_{MM'}$, and $g(\Gamma) \mapsto g^J_{MM'}$, then $(f \star g)(\Gamma) \mapsto h^J_{MM'}$, where

$$h^J_{MM"} = \sum_{k=-J}^{J} f^J_{Mk}\, g^J_{kM'}.$$

This equation can be interpreted as follows. The Fourier coefficients of any function $f(\Gamma)$ can be arranged in the form of an (infinite) block-diagonal matrix, where the J-th block has the dimensions $(2J+1) \times (2J+1)$ and contains the coefficients $f^J_{MM'}$. The coefficients of the convolution of two functions are simply obtained via the matrix multiplication of the original coefficient matrices.

Finally, if the coefficient matrices corresponding to the Fourier transform of functions $\rho(\hat{\imath}, \hat{o}, \Gamma, \mu)$ and $q(\Gamma, \mu)$ are $R(\hat{\imath}, \hat{o}, \mu)$ and $Q(\mu)$, respectively, then the relation Eq. (5.3) assumes the following form:

$$\Big(\partial_\mu R(\hat{\imath}, \hat{o}, \mu)\Big) \cdot Q(\mu) + R(\hat{\imath}, \hat{o}, \mu) \cdot \partial_\mu Q(\mu) = 0. \qquad (5.4)$$

For the J-th block of coefficients, Eq. (5.4) represents a closed system of $(2J+1) \times (2J+1)$ linear differential equations on the same number of functions of μ. The solution of such homogeneous linear differential equations are straightforward and involve matrix exponentials. In other words, this system can be solved numerically in each block, and we can solve it up to any fixed maximum cutoff frequency J.

6 Nearly-specular reflection

Let us consider the isotropic case and assume that each microfacet at the scale μ_0 is a perfect mirror, and that the surface at the scale μ is completely flat:

$$\rho(\hat{\imath}, \hat{o}, \vec{m}, \mu_0) \sim \delta(\vec{m} - \vec{m}_s(\hat{\imath}, \hat{o})), \quad \text{and} \quad p(\vec{m}_\infty, \vec{m}, \mu) \sim \delta(\vec{m} - \vec{m}_\infty).$$

Then Eq. (4.4) leads to the the following statement:

$$R(\hat{\imath}, \hat{o}, \vec{W}, \mu) = Q(\vec{W}, \mu_0) F \tag{6.1}$$

with some phase factor F. Eq. (6.1) represents a well-known relation between the metal surface roughness and its BRDF [Har86], but it also means, that starting from a trivial BRDF, one may prepare arbitrary BRDFs using special micro-structured surfaces.

In particular, let us imagine a surface whose normal vector distribution $p(\vec{m}_\infty, \vec{m}, \mu_0) = h(\|\vec{m}_\infty - \vec{m}\|)$ is given by the following generalized function:

$$h(x) = \left[\frac{\log^n x}{x}\right]_+,$$

whose action on some probe function $\psi(x)$ is given by

$$\langle h, \psi \rangle = \int_0^\infty \frac{\log^n x}{x} \left(\psi(x) - \psi(0)\right) dx.$$

Such "plus-distributions" are well-known in particle physics, where they describe scattering at small angles. Via Eq. (6.1), they may enter the BRDFs and give rise to exotic "nearly-specular" kind of reflection, which is neither specular, nor diffuse. The corresponding contributions for each exponent n may be measured and characterized by the dedicated experiments, and used to improve the stability of BRDF measurements[2].

So far, this "nearly-specular" reflection remains a theoretical prediction in a need of further research.

[2] It is possible that the surfaces exhibiting such "near-specular" reflection are relatively common, but its contributions have always been confused with the specular or the diffuse components, leading to non-reproducible results and poor agreement with theoretical expectations.

7 Summary

In this report, we have demonstrated how the BRDFs may be adjusted to the observation scale of a specific scene and detector setup, and derived a general evolution equation. We have further demonstrated a closed-form solution of the evolution equation in the isotropic case, and suggested a simple way to integrate the anisotropic evolution up to any finite angular frequency. Finally, we demonstrated a mechanism that may generate arbitrary contributions to BRDFs via special surface micro-structures, and hypothesized the existence of the novel "nearly-specular" type of reflection.

In the future, we plan to verify the presented equations with the real and simulated experiments, and extend the evolution to a more general class of surfaces (e.g., to those exhibiting significant microscopic masking and shading). We also plan to implement the evolution-based tools for computer graphics and BRDF measurements.

Bibliography

[Bas01] Michael Bass. *Handbook of optics, Volumes 1-2*. McGraw-Hill, 2 edition, 2001.

[Har86] J. E. Harvey. Light-scattering characteristics of optical surfaces. Proc. SPIE 645, pages 107 – 115, 1986.

[KR08] Peter J. Kostelec and Daniel N. Rockmore. FFTs on the rotation group. *Journal of Fourier Analysis and Applications*, 14:145 – 179, 2008.

[TLQ+02] Ping Tan, Stephen Lin, Long Quan, Baining Guo, and Heung-Yeung Shum. Filtering and rendering of resolution-dependent reflectance models. *IEEE Transactions on Visualization and Computer Graphics*, 1:1 – 14, 2002.

[Wen10] Jakob Wenzel. Mitsuba renderer, 2010. http://www.mitsuba-renderer.org.

Karlsruher Schriftenreihe zur Anthropomatik (ISSN 1863-6489)

Herausgeber: Prof. Dr.-Ing. Jürgen Beyerer

Band 1 Jürgen Geisler
Leistung des Menschen am Bildschirmarbeitsplatz. 2006
ISBN 3-86644-070-7

Band 2 Elisabeth Peinsipp-Byma
Leistungserhöhung durch Assistenz in interaktiven Systemen zur Szenenanalyse. 2007
ISBN 978-3-86644-149-1

Band 3 Jürgen Geisler, Jürgen Beyerer (Hrsg.)
Mensch-Maschine-Systeme. 2010
ISBN 978-3-86644-457-7

Band 4 Jürgen Beyerer, Marco Huber (Hrsg.)
Proceedings of the 2009 Joint Workshop of Fraunhofer IOSB and Institute for Anthropomatics, Vision and Fusion Laboratory. 2010
ISBN 978-3-86644-469-0

Band 5 Thomas Usländer
Service-oriented design of environmental information systems. 2010
ISBN 978-3-86644-499-7

Band 6 Giulio Milighetti
Multisensorielle diskret-kontinuierliche Überwachung und Regelung humanoider Roboter. 2010
ISBN 978-3-86644-568-0

Band 7 Jürgen Beyerer, Marco Huber (Hrsg.)
Proceedings of the 2010 Joint Workshop of Fraunhofer IOSB and Institute for Anthropomatics, Vision and Fusion Laboratory. 2011
ISBN 978-3-86644-609-0

Band 8 Eduardo Monari
Dynamische Sensorselektion zur auftragsorientierten Objektverfolgung in Kameranetzwerken. 2011
ISBN 978-3-86644-729-5

Die Bände sind unter www.ksp.kit.edu als PDF frei verfügbar oder als Druckausgabe bestellbar.

Band 9 Thomas Bader
Multimodale Interaktion in Multi-Display-Umgebungen. 2011
ISBN 3-86644-760-8

Band 10 Christian Frese
Planung kooperativer Fahrmanöver für kognitive Automobile. 2012
ISBN 978-3-86644-798-1

Band 11 Jürgen Beyerer, Alexey Pak (Hrsg.)
Proceedings of the 2011 Joint Workshop of Fraunhofer IOSB and Institute for Anthropomatics, Vision and Fusion Laboratory. 2012
ISBN 978-3-86644-855-1

Band 12 Miriam Schleipen
Adaptivität und Interoperabilität von Manufacturing Execution Systemen (MES). 2013
ISBN 978-3-86644-955-8

Band 13 Jürgen Beyerer, Alexey Pak (Hrsg.)
Proceedings of the 2012 Joint Workshop of Fraunhofer IOSB and Institute for Anthropomatics, Vision and Fusion Laboratory. 2013
ISBN 978-3-86644-988-6

Band 14 Hauke-Hendrik Vagts
Privatheit und Datenschutz in der intelligenten Überwachung: Ein datenschutzgewährendes System, entworfen nach dem „Privacy by Design" Prinzip. 2013
ISBN 978-3-7315-0041-4

Band 15 Christian Kühnert
Data-driven Methods for Fault Localization in Process Technology. 2013
ISBN 978-3-7315-0098-8

Band 16 Alexander Bauer
Probabilistische Szenenmodelle für die Luftbildauswertung. 2014
ISBN 978-3-7315-0167-1

Band 17 Jürgen Beyerer, Alexey Pak (Hrsg.)
Proceedings of the 2013 Joint Workshop of Fraunhofer IOSB and Institute for Anthropomatics, Vision and Fusion Laboratory. 2014
ISBN 978-3-7315-0212-8

Band 18 Michael Teutsch
Moving Object Detection and Segmentation for Remote Aerial Video Surveillance. 2015
ISBN 978-3-7315-0320-0

Band 19 Marco Huber
Nonlinear Gaussian Filtering: Theory, Algorithms, and Applications. 2015
ISBN 978-3-7315-0338-5

Band 20 Jürgen Beyerer, Alexey Pak (Hrsg.)
Proceedings of the 2014 Joint Workshop of Fraunhofer IOSB and Institute for Anthropomatics, Vision and Fusion Laboratory. 2014
ISBN 978-3-7315-0401-6

Band 21 Todor Dimitrov
Permanente Optimierung dynamischer Probleme der Fertigungssteuerung unter Einbeziehung von Benutzerinteraktionen. 2015
ISBN 978-3-7315-0426-9

Band 22 Benjamin Kühn
Interessengetriebene audiovisuelle Szenenexploration. 2016
ISBN 978-3-7315-0457-3

Band 23 Yvonne Fischer
Wissensbasierte probabilistische Modellierung für die Situationsanalyse am Beispiel der maritimen Überwachung. 2016
ISBN 978-3-7315-0460-3

Band 24 Jürgen Beyerer, Alexey Pak (Hrsg.)
Proceedings of the 2015 Joint Workshop of Fraunhofer IOSB and Institute for Anthropomatics, Vision and Fusion Laboratory. 2016
ISBN 978-3-7315-0519-8

Band 25 Pascal Birnstill
Privacy-Respecting Smart Video Surveillance Based on Usage Control Enforcement. 2016
ISBN 978-3-7315-0538-9

Band 26 Philipp Woock
Umgebungskartenschätzung aus Sidescan-Sonardaten für ein autonomes Unterwasserfahrzeug. 2016
ISBN 978-3-7315-0541-9

Band 27 Janko Petereit
Adaptive State × Time Lattices: A Contribution to Mobile Robot Motion Planning in Unstructured Dynamic Environments. 2017
ISBN 978-3-7315-0580-8

Band 28 Erik Ludwig Krempel
Steigerung der Akzeptanz von intelligenter Video-überwachung in öffentlichen Räumen. 2017
ISBN 978-3-7315-0598-3

Band 29 Jürgen Moßgraber
Ein Rahmenwerk für die Architektur von Frühwarnsystemen. 2017
ISBN 978-3-7315-0638-6

Band 30 Andrey Belkin
World Modeling for Intelligent Autonomous Systems. 2017
ISBN 978-3-7315-0641-6

Band 31 Chettapong Janya-Anurak
Framework for Analysis and Identification of Nonlinear Distributed Parameter Systems using Bayesian Uncertainty Quantification based on Generalized Polynomial Chaos. 2017
ISBN 978-3-7315-0642-3

Band 32 David Münch
Begriffliche Situationsanalyse aus Videodaten bei unvollständiger und fehlerhafter Information. 2017
ISBN 978-3-7315-0644-7

Band 33 Jürgen Beyerer, Alexey Pak (Eds.)
Proceedings of the 2016 Joint Workshop of Fraunhofer IOSB and Institute for Anthropomatics, Vision and Fusion Laboratory. 2017
ISBN 978-3-7315-0678-2